What Are Children Learning "about" Islam and the Middle East in Public Schools?

Are the Students Also Being Taught to Hate America?

By

David Pimentel

June 14, 2011

Order this book online at www.trafford.com
or email orders@trafford.com

Most Trafford titles are also available at major online book retailers.

Printed in the United States of America.

ISBN: 978-1-4269-7469-4 (sc)
ISBN: 978-1-4269-7470-0 (hc)
ISBN: 978-1-4269-7471-7 (e)

Library of Congress Control Number: 2011911171

Trafford rev. 06/30/2011

 www.trafford.com

North America & international
toll-free: 1 888 232 4444 (USA & Canada)
phone: 250 383 6864 ♦ fax: 812 355 4082

No Time to Waste

Due to the urgency and gravity of danger of what is being done in our public schools and colleges, in Hollywood, and what is not being done by the media or our government, I have had to reduce the sources of material which are included in this book. The situation is urgent because many other authors and writers have attempted to wake up America to what is happening in our own country and those attempts have not appeared to make any difference in school or government policies that will be discussed here. This country is in grave danger because its enemies are many, but the greatest are those who are wearing suits and ties so as not to appear threatening or suspicious. I will do my best to explain and demonstrate how the public schools, Hollywood, the government and others may be teaching our children to hate America and allowing our enemies to infiltrate the school system with open arms.

Surely a strong nation like America could resist and defeat an enemy such as terrorists who are supported and funded by foreign governments. Likewise, America, with the most powerful military in the world, should have no problem controlling or defeating any threat from countries such as Russia and China. Although it may be more difficult, the United States should also be able to overcome any covert operation that attempts to infiltrate various governmental agencies in order to change policymaking which makes it easier to undermine and attack the country from within. However, is America, with all its efforts to be tolerant and compassionate, strong enough to defeat all of its enemies all at once? I hope and pray that America will still be standing strong long after its enemies have been crushed and subdued, but currently the leadership appears to be lacking in courage to confront the enemies of freedom and liberty. The present excuses range from not wanting to offend anyone or anyone's religion to the belief that America has had its time of becoming rich on the backs of other nations and peoples, but that time is over now.

Actually, it should come as no surprise that America is under attack from so many enemies, but at least one would think that some reporter or public leader would have the guts to stand up and tell the general public of the real and present danger they are in. Unfortunately, the people are continually reminded by the current president that the economic crisis is over and that the recovery has begun. The average American just shakes their head in disbelief because they see all the empty homes and business offices around town, as well as all the homeless and unemployed walking the streets aimlessly or standing on a corner waiting for a contractor to pick them up for work. The last president was not much better as he simply instructed the public to "just keep shopping" so the economy will stay strong. That was probably the first time in history that during the time of war a nation's leader, rather than calling its citizens to prepare for war and hard times, told the citizens to simply keep shopping. I suppose the situation in Rome was similar as their leader told the musicians to keep playing the music as the empire collapsed to the ground.

As I said before, I hope and pray that America can withstand the multi-pronged attack from within and without, but if those who are sworn to defend the constitution and the country are aligned with those who hate this country, then the citizens are left with no choice but to fight on their own. The best and brightest soldiers are fighting and "building" in other nations while the greatest and richest nation on earth is left wide open for assault and invasion. Sadly, many of these brave and strong soldiers are dying or returning home without some of their limbs simply because of some simple electronic device and their vehicles are not built strong enough to endure such an explosion. Perhaps the Americans should ignore the U.N. like the Israelis did and use Caterpillar bulldozers to roam around a specific area. I know that each and every (almost every) American soldier would defend and die for their country, especially since that is exactly what they swore to do, but I know that once a person enters the military, they are trained to follow the chain of command and follow orders. Thus, it could be heart-wrenching for a soldier to reach the conclusion that he or she should stand with the people rather than stand down and watch as the people are led astray by its own government or foreign entities or both.

The reason I wrote this book is because each American must make an important choice and decision. Everybody has to decide whether they want to pro-American or anti-American. It should be obvious which side I picked. But I guess it depends on how a person is raised. I was raised to have good manners, respect others, to defend myself and others who are being picked on, to respect my elders and to love this country. I learned that many people, including some of my relatives, died so this country could grow and become strong. So who am I that I should show any disrespect or lack of appreciation for what many others before me built and died for? Yet some Americans, including the current leadership, were taught differently. They were taught that America became rich because of slavery and that America is racist because white Europeans sit in positions of power. (They never mention that Greece, Assyria, Rome and nearly every culture had slaves and that only America and a few others have been courageous enough to abolish it.) They were taught that communism is better because it redistributes the wealth equally among the people. (They never mention the millions killed by communist leaders.) They were taught that America should experience poverty and despair like every other country. (They never mention that America provides financial aid to every poor country or that the dictators and warlords keep all the money and aid for themselves while the masses suffer in hunger and hopelessness.) After all, why should America or Americans be exempt from all the turmoil and suffering that other countries have to experience? (They always forget to mention how generous Americans are in donating money, aid and food to many countries around the world, especially after a natural disaster has occurred.)

As you can see, I love this country. I know I was fortunate to be born here. I know I was blessed with parents who provided for me and my siblings. I know that I am privileged to be able to visit and see the wonder of God's creation here in America. I know many others have traveled much more than me, but I have enjoyed the grandeur of Yosemite National Park and many of its surroundings. I have had the privilege of visiting Idaho and seeing the beauty of its many landscapes and rivers. Living in California all of my life, I have seen the great and spectacular west coast beaches, from San Diego and Malibu to Monterey and Vancouver. I have not seen the rest of the world, but I have no need to since I know the God who made it all. Like all of creation, all good things come to an end. I wish that Americans could enjoy their barbecues, surfing, skiing, hiking, bicycling and any other form of recreation for generations to come, but nothing lasts forever.

Although my words may seem to be full of pessimism as I point out the various attacks America is experiencing, I am truly thankful to be alive now. In the same way that I have made important decisions regarding what I believe and who I put my trust in, everyone else will have the opportunity to make their choices under pressure as well. America has experienced many tough trials throughout its grand history, but its citizens are facing very difficult challenges as each and every crisis seems to be getting more and more personal. While no one wishes to experience a crisis, it is true that personal character and growth does occur more often when one is being put to the test. Yes, some are stronger than others, but all of us are fragile and mortal beings. So there should be no shame in recognizing that we cannot survive or succeed on our own. In fact, those times of helplessness are usually the only times we consider that we need the help of God. I have been down many times and I know that my experience is common to man and women, so I am confident that Americans, rich and poor alike, are going to need each other in the days ahead. America and Americans are under serious attack these days. However, many Americans do not even know it. This is another reason why I wrote this book, because I think it is only fair for those who are involved in a fight to at least know that they are in a fight. Otherwise, anyone caught by surprise is likely to be unprepared for any battle, and I do not think that is right. So I pray for all parents who have the awesome responsibility of raising their children to be happy and healthy adults, especially during these difficult and trying times. And I hope that the information contained in this book helps parents and others figure out what they need to do to make their children more safe and secure. Because no matter what color you are, how rich you are or what religion you believe in, the simple reality is that America is under attack and you need to think about what (besides shopping) you can do about it.

CHAPTER ONE

Is there an anti-American message in Avatar?

I know that Avatar was quite an entertaining movie and that millions were amazed by the special effects. I also am aware that a recent movie might not be the best way to begin a book about how students are being taught to hate or dislike their own country. However, since their beginnings, movies and entertainment have been a very effective means of propaganda and persuasion. As a result, I believe a discussion of the hit movie is an excellent starting point in demonstrating how viewers can be introduced or encouraged to have a particular opinion on events portrayed in the movie. Thus, makers of movies can present many various messages to the audience, knowing that most of the audience will be receptive to such messages because they merely want to be entertained and not concerned about political slants or agendas. So I would like to briefly discuss this great movie production by James Cameron and raise the issue of whether or not political messages were included intentionally.

There is no argument that Avatar was a one-of-a-kind movie with all the spectacular colors and special effects that boggled the mind. I believe one of the main reasons that Avatar was such a big hit is because of the way it was introduced and advertised to the public audience. I am a frequent viewer to the movie cinema, so I remember vividly the first preview of Avatar. I was not too impressed with the bright blue characters but I knew that some people would enjoy the special effects. However, after the second and third preview, I was curious and interested because one of the main characters was in the military. The preview also drew upon the sympathy of potential viewers because the soldier was paralyzed from the waist down. Having seen that, how could I simply turn away and dismiss this new and unheard of movie? The previews were having the desired and positive effect on my thought and emotional processes. As it turned out, I was not the only one being slowly but surely attracted to the movie.

Besides being a simply amazing movie that presented a new and different type of production, did Avatar include a political message? If so, what was the message? Was the movie going to be supportive of the military or cast a shadow on its mission? Was the movie making a statement regarding America's involvement in past or current wars? Of course, I could not answer these questions until I actually saw the movie. The advertisers for the movie were very successful and the previews were effective. The hype was growing and everybody was talking about going to see the movie. The previews had definitely grabbed my attention, but a red flag went up as I saw the wounded soldier being changed and making the decision to fight against his fellow troops. As a red flag usually indicates, perhaps this new hi-tech, sci-fi, and partially animated movie was intended to be more than just an entertaining production.

As the release date approached, I began hearing rumors about the movie. With the U.S. military involved in the wars in Iraq and Afghanistan, there seemed to be a growing and questioning sentiment that American soldiers should be brought home. Like many Americans, I knew young men who had graduated from West Point and were then immediately sent to one of the wars, only to be sent home with a notice to their parents that their son or daughter was killed in combat. No matter what political party we belong to, nobody wants to see the lives of our finest young men and women end prematurely. As you can see, I would have no problem if Avatar was a great movie simply because it had great special effects and was a sci-fi movie about something that will never happen in real life. However, if Avatar was truly an indictment on America and its military, then I would have to ask why.

To be fair to the writer of Avatar, many movies are used as political propaganda. So I suppose I would be totally amazed and surprised if a movie was great on its own merits and had no political slant. However, I would like to occasionally see a movie that supports the American military and its values rather than being made to feel guilty because I love and admire this country. For instance, could someone make a movie that tells about how America and Americans reach out to assist many people who have suffered from a natural disaster such as the earthquakes in Thailand and Haiti? More recently, two days after the major earthquake and tsunami that hit Japan, the United States sent eight ships to provide supplies and first aid to those in need. What other country does this and offers free assistance to foreign countries and people who have just experienced a natural disaster? Did Iran, Saudi Arabia or North Korea offer such assistance? What other country can devise such an easy way of donating funds to hurting people where the average citizen can make a ten dollar donation simply by texting a specific number? Perhaps the texting is misused or abused by the voting for American Idol candidates, but at least Americans can use the same method to donate money to the Red Cross or other organizations that provide much needed assistance to those in need, especially when their homes and lives have been shattered by a hurricane or an earthquake.

Speaking of America's generosity, what other country provides protection and lavish quarters for members of the United Nations and treats them like Kings and Queens? What other country gives monetary and humanitarian aid to virtually every poor country? The U.S. is so generous that it makes such donations a part of its annual budget. I think that makes America exceptional! What does our president say when asked if he believes in American exceptionalism? The president says that he believes in American exceptionalism in much the same way that Greece believes in Greek exceptionalism or that China believes in Chinese exceptionalism. Well, no wonder that our children do not think that America is such a great country for doing so many great things. At least the president's wife is finally proud of her country. I am also glad that the principal-in-chief has finally spoken out against bullying in our schools. Wait, I do not want to wander too much off track.

Why can't anyone in Hollywood write a movie about the Presidents or other great American leaders? I am glad to see so many documentaries and other specials on the History Channel about people who have become rich and famous because they created a great product, such as Colonel Sanders or other individuals who now have a chain of fast-food restaurants. It is very interesting, entertaining and inspiring to learn about ordinary people who can start a small a small business because of a need and then watch it grow as the years go by, such as the Hiltons or the owners of the railroad companies. Everyone likes to read or watch a story about people who have become successful.

So why aren't there any major movies about George Washington and others who did and gave so much for the birth of this great country? There are some good books about early American history and how the Revolution against England came about, but who are the audience of these books? Adults, people who already have some knowledge of what the early Americans endured and sacrificed for the endeavor and survival of the new experiment and idea called America. What about the potential audience of children and students? Are there any comic books or movies or video games about the experiences of the early Americans and their many struggles and failures? Yes, of course, there are many boring textbooks on the subject that are presented to our children and students. This is yet another reason why so many children are turned off about our rich American history. Who wants to read and learn about history when the teacher keeps writing dates and names on the blackboard and then expects everyone to remember the statistics and information and do well on the exams? Finally, some universities are providing prospective teachers with new and exciting materials and projects to teach the subjects to students so that the children are not so bored and looking forward to break and recess.

I suppose entertainment and education are two separate areas of expertise. Yet that has not stopped Hollywood from attempting to and succeeding at teaching millions of children about their version or opinion on what has taken place in American history and why. Although "Waiting for Superman" has received good reviews for its criticism of the current state of public education, it is still a documentary and not a movie that captures and maintains the attention of the young population. There are some great comic books and movies about superheroes, but everyone knows they are merely fantasy figures and that no one person or character can save the world from evil. Except for Jesus Christ, that is. But we can't teach the children and students about him, can we? No, wait. Now schools can teach *about* religion, such as Islam, but information about any other religion is still considered indoctrination and the establishment of a religion.

So, am I the only person who thinks that there was a political message in Avatar? Not at all. With Avatar being such a blockbuster movie, there were many different types of reviews on the colorful movie, but I selected only the most appropriate review that is somewhat easy for a laymen like myself to understand. Some reviews included discussion of a political message. However, some had unique commentaries and questions that I had not considered after watching the movie. Before sharing the review, I would just like to make the point that the Pandora woman named Neytiri looked much more like one of my favorite actresses, Uma Thurman, than the actual actress, Zoe Saldana. I could write a chapter on Thurman, but she is not the current subject of discussion. So on to the review.

In his review of Avatar, Roz Kaveney noted that the Pandoran biosphere is literally a great and intelligent being and that the Pandorans dwell in the presence of their god Eywa. After reading Kaveney's comments, I remembered that the blue characters from Pandora referred to Eywa as "Mother" and that they worshipped Eywa with their chanting while kneeling down by the sacred tree. Members of the audience likely experienced different responses when watching such a unique form of chanting, but I quickly formulated my own opinion of what was going on. My first reaction to the chanting was that it sounded much like the chanting of a cult as they reach a hypnotic state in which the cult members become unaware of all else that is happening around them. I can recall of similar scenes that took place in the Pirates of the Caribbean movies and in documentaries about the Aztecs that were on the History Channel. Each time I have seen such a scene, the warriors or cult members were preparing for either war or a human sacrifice. In Avatar, it could be said that the Pandorans were preparing for both. They were preparing for battle with the "sky people" and they were also trying to get Jake out of their territory because they felt he had betrayed them.

Roz Kaveney's review also made me recall one of the curious quotes from the movie which I knew at the time would be worth recalling. Kaveney mentioned that Jake was allowed to remain in Pandora because one of the sacred trees had indicated that Jake should be trusted by causing the white pods to fall and remain on him. This comment by Kaveney raised in my mind the issue of trust. Did the Pandorans trust Jake because of the "sign" given by the tree or did they finally trust him after he helped them defeat the strong military of the "sky people"? The reason I ask this question is because of the many wars and conflicts that are going on in the world today. Despite the efforts and funds spent on diplomacy, does any nation or people really trust an opposing party as they negotiate or do they only accept the other party after the party has conceded and agrees with their particular worldview or beliefs?

I also had a question about the "sacred" trees of Pandora or
any other form of nature worship. What does the tree or any
other inanimate object of worship do for the worshippers? In
Avatar, what did the tree do for the Pandorans beside provide an
extravagant light show and the false idea that all things are as
one in the futuristic utopia? Like any utopia, it never truly exists
and is merely one's imagination. Was Pandora a place of utopia,
even without the presence of the sky people or any other modern
military threat? Not likely, since they were trained warriors and
always prepared for a battle. Who did they fight with before
the appearance of the sky people? Like Native Americans, they
probably fought other tribes in nearby regions or whoever was a
threat to their territory. Sounds like the behavior of most, if not
all, the different cultures and nations of people who have ever
existed on earth. Ever since Cain killed his brother Abel, man
has been at war against other men. If brother can kill brother
over jealousy and affection, then it should be no surprise that man
is still at war with other men all around the world. However,
America, or at least the leadership of America, seems oblivious to
the idea that some other nation or culture could pose a real threat
to its existence and freedom. America is at war here at home, not
just in Iraq and Afghanistan, but each time there is some act of
violence taken against Americans or its soldiers in America, the
leaders speak as if they are damage control employees for a large
company rather than someone who is concerned for the safety of
American citizens. More on that subject later.

Kaveney also made another interesting comment on the
Avatar movie when he mentioned that "the most important and
telling criticism leveled at the film, even causing some people to
boycott it, is that the central plot structure is a neo-colonist one,
in which the Pandorans need the help of a superior being, a white
American, to survive", and thus, the story is about him rather
than the Pandorans. If Kaveney is correct in his analysis of the
movie's critics, then that would mean that not only was there an

anti-America message included in the movie, but that also some potential viewers would boycott the movie because of their anti-white sentiments. Although Kaveney attempts to explain that Jake is not only the Great White Savior, but that he is also the man who had to learn many things from the Pandorans, especially from Neytiri his personal guide. I disagree with Kaveney on that point because I see the movie more as a conversion story. I conclude that the Na'vi won the war against the sky people because the Na'vi convinced the white American that he needed to change his ways or else he would just be another robotic soldier serving his evil master, the American military. Remember, America bad and wrong, and everyone else good and right!

One final comment about the review by Roz Kaveney, I liked the way he noted the similarity of Pandora having two trees in the same way that Christianity thought does, namely the cross and the tree of knowledge in the Garden of Eden. Kaveney graciously acknowledged that the tree of Eden was where the fall of man occurred whereas the redemption of man took place on the cross. Kaveney also stated that he did not know if James Cameron was an atheist or not, but that Cameron could not resist the mythic story that fit so well in Avatar. I agree that the mythic story is good because it is one that is often included in movies that involve an epic struggle. The story line also is common as it helps the audience see the movie as a story between good and evil. In Avatar, the Pandora represents the good people and the American military represent the evil people. Apparently, Cameron's depiction and message was effective as many reviews mentioned that the movie crowds cheered as Jake and the Pandorans defeated the evil sky people. I did not see the movie in a theatre so I cannot attest to that crowd reaction as I watched the final scenes. However, I can imagine such a reaction occurring as the evil military and business people were attempting to steal the treasure from Pandora. It would not be too difficult to persuade the audience that this is exactly what happened in world history and that is how the United

States became so rich and powerful. This message of anti-America is also being taught in the classrooms of America as students are learning that American business owners became successful and wealthy on the backs of slaves who did all the dirty work while the owners drank tea and lived in mansions. There is no mention that slavery was a common practice in most countries at the time and that America is the only country that has abolished slavery. But schools don't want America students to be sympathetic and understanding toward their founding fathers while the rest of the world is being taught that America is the great evil empire.

The anti-America message is also very modern and up to date as the United States wages war in Middle Eastern countries where terrorists who are smuggled into other countries and funded by Iran are called insurgents and Americans are regarded as the terrible invaders. Again, there was no outcry when Saddam Hussein killed enemies and his own people with mustard gas and buried them in mass graves. It seems that the U.S. military is doomed and to be condemned whether it chooses to take action or no action in foreign affairs and atrocities. For instance, some critics did not want the American military to get involved in Iraq or Afghanistan after 9/11, but they eagerly sought American military assistance when recent protesters were being killed in Libya. Actually, some critics did not sympathize with America whatsoever after 9/11, but instead chose to justify the terrorist attacks carried out by the militant Muslims, mostly from Saudi Arabia. Similarly, critics cried out for U.S. help as people were being slaughtered in Rhawanda, but not in Somalia or other countries where warlords were killing unarmed citizens and children. Now that individuals from the U.N. have used American and other western weaponry to force a no-fly zone in Libya, perhaps these same people such as Samantha Power and others can demand a no-pirate zone where innocent civilians are being hijacked, kidnapped and killed while traveling or conducting business.

As you can see, it is difficult and nearly impossible to please the many different factions that exist in America, especially when some groups strongly support the military and U.S. sovereignty while others seem to denounce the military and eagerly wait for the Americans to with the international community as one. With presidents declaring that there is a New World Order and constant rhetoric about a global community, the momentum appears to be with those who desire a weaker America so that things can be more equal and fair. These groups and individuals fail to mention that no other dominant or powerful country in world history has surrendered their sovereignty for the sake of making things fair and equal. As usual, the leaders of such groups do not set a good example for their followers. For instance, why does Al Gore continue to fly his personal jets while demanding that the "common" person drive a battery-run vehicle? Why do the rich and elite want average Americans to live with regulations that control the amount of water and electricity they use while the elite enjoy their mansions?

These same anti-America groups do not want America youth and students to be reminded that nearly every country in the world is governed by a dictator and that most "citizens of the world" do not enjoy the freedom that Americans have. One may even wonder why these anti-America people continue to live in a country that they despise so much, but the explanation is easy when it is discovered that their tactic is to destroy the country from within since they are unable to do so from outside the country. Hence, a great and spectacular movie like Avatar is rightly praised for its special effects and vision, but unfortunately, the highly successful movie also includes an anti-America message that supports the current trend of bearing contempt for America, its military and its values. Many people and groups promote the "It's a small world after all" message, but this false illusion can be quickly discounted and ignored when one learns about the turmoil and distress that takes place in nearly every country on a daily basis, not just when there is a protest shown on CNN.

CHAPTER 2

What is being taught in America's public schools?

When I was in elementary school, the only things I remember were the pretty girls and the lunch food. I had the usual crush on a couple of girls, actually three girls. Two of the girls were twins who were five feet and ten inches tall in 6th grade. I am not sure if they were actually that tall, but it sure seemed like to me because I was only about three feet tall in 5th grade. Fortunately, I experienced a major growth spurt in junior high. Then I was a little taller than four feet. There were quite a few beautiful girls in junior high, but I was still shorter than most of them. Okay, I was shorter than all of them. However, there was one major change that occurred in my life from elementary to junior high school. I no longer was concerned about the lunch food as I became active in various sports in the P.E. class. I may have been small, but I was born with the gift of speed and strength, especially for my size. There were a couple of other boys who were as short as I was, but one of them was much stronger. His name was Robert and his arms were like Popeye's. I believe he got his physical strength from his dad because his father appeared as if he could lift a car engine out of a car with one arm. He was a good friend all through elementary and high school.

So what's the point of all this? The point is that most middle school students may not remember the academic areas of study, but they might very well remember if they were being taught a new and different religion. I don't remember being taught about any religion in school, but I was taught religion in catechism after school. I suppose the school system was successful since I was able to find employment right after I graduated. A few of my friends could not read that well, but they too were able to find a job in the construction business. Actually, they made a lot more money than working in a nice clean office. Back then, I guess the main job of the school was to teach students the basic skills of reading, writing and arithmetic. As I said, schools were considered successful as almost everyone graduated and became employed. My generation was a fortunate one as I don't recall anyone not being able to find a job except for during the rainy season. Even when they received unemployment checks, the construction workers made much more than I did. But everything in life seemed to be okay. Why wouldn't it be, the Eagles and Fleetwood Mac were making a lot of good albums!

So anyway, back to the school environment. It was safe most of the time. Sure there were fights, but back then one person won and one person lost and that was the end of it. Now, I guess if someone wins, the loser goes and gets four or five of his buddies and then jumps the winner. Well, so much for the good old days. Remember, when a child is in school, all they are concerned about is their small little world which includes lots of friends and memories. Although President Kennedy, Martin Luther King and Robert Kennedy were shot and killed while I was in school, those tragedies seemed like a dream or like something that happened on the other side of the world. I remember riding my bike to go see Robert Kennedy as he stopped in Modesto on his way to Los Angeles, where he would be assassinated later that same terrible day. I remember thinking to myself as I watched the news that night, "I just saw him, I just saw him." Back then, boys were not supposed to cry. So I went to my room and cried later when nobody was around.

As other major events were happening in the world, such as the Vietnam War and numerous protests on college campuses because of the war and draft, I was still mainly concerned with the latest hits like Hotel California or "Baby, I love your way" by

Peter Frampton. There was some minor news regarding school
that I recall taking place in the 1960's and 1970's. Prayer and
the Bible were banned from public schools. I guess it was 1962
and 1963 to be exact. Some group was arguing in the courts that
these Christian ideas should be banned because of the separation
of church and state clause in the constitution. I am not sure
if that was when I first became interested in the law, but I still
haven't found that separation clause. The times are definitely
changing. Apparently, that same clause was somehow only meant
to apply to Christian beliefs and values. I have recently discovered
that another growing and expanding religion has been provided
with a free pass and rather than be banned from public schools
like Christianity, the religion is actually being promoted and
supported. Oh ACLU, where did you go? Oh ACLU, where are
you when atheists are demanding that religion be banned and
struck from the public schools? I wonder why the atheists are not
crying out and complaining and filing lawsuits against this "new
and popular" religion that has been given such a respectable place
in our schools? Perhaps many parents, even atheist parents, are
not aware that this certain religion is being promoted in public
schools today. Well, they are going to find out about it now.

Let's examine a case where a federal judge stated that a Contra
Costa school was merely teaching seventh graders about Islam
and not indoctrinating them by having the students role-play in
their history class. In a 2003 article, the SFGate reported that
the history class called for students to adopt Muslim names and
recite language from prayers. The article continued by reporting
that U.S. District Judge Phyllis Hamilton dismissed the suit by
two students and their parents who claimed that the role-playing
amounted to an unconstitutional endorsement of Islam. The
article further reported that the teacher encouraged the students
to use Muslim names, recite prayers in class, required students to
recite a line from a prayer and made them give up something for
a day to simulate fasting during the Islamic Ramadan.

Maybe judges and rulings change over the years because they are only human, but hopefully the decisions that affect all the children in public schools are not altered due to political pressure or attachments. On their website, Americans United state that it is important for public schools to protect parental rights, and thus decisions "about" religion belong with the family. I wholeheartedly agree with those statements. Americans United also mention that in 1963 the Supreme Court handed down a very important ruling involving prayer in public schools, which declared that school-sponsored Bible reading and recitation of the Lord's Prayer is unconstitutional. The case was Abington Township School District v. Schemp. The AU is quick to clarify that prayer is still allowed in schools as long as the students pray on their own and the school does not sponsor such prayer. I also agree with these statements and interpretation of the Supreme Court decision. So perhaps parents need to pursue legal action in removing any form of prayer or the reciting of Muslim prayers based on the ruling which came from the Schemp case.

In my humble opinion, I think that public schools allowing or requiring students to recite Muslim prayers in a classroom setting is legally the same as having a class or the entire school read the Bible or recite the Lord's Prayer. Is not the school sponsoring the Islamic prayers the same way that schools formerly sponsored the recital of the Lord's Prayer? By requiring students to recite Muslim prayers during school hours during a time of instruction that is funded by taxpayer funds, I do believe that the schools are indeed sponsoring such prayer. As such, the recital or memorization of any religious prayer, including Islamic, should be considered unconstitutional and therefore discontinued at once. It should not matter whether the students who are required to recite such prayers are attending public schools in California, Arizona or any other state in America. It should not matter whether a school board, school district, teacher or publisher thinks that Islamic prayers should be allowed because it would be a gesture of tolerance. The law is the same for everybody. In this case, the law pertains to every religion. I do not know if business in the public school system is done the same way as it is in Washington D. C., but no group should be allowed to influence a textbook publisher regarding what is and is not included in a textbook.

Back to the Byron School District case, let's hear what the principal of the school in question had to say about the lessons on Islam in the classroom. According to an article in World Net Daily, the principal of Excelsior, Nancie Castro, explained that the role-playing and simulation games are common teaching practices used in other subjects as well. These role-playing activities may well be used in other topics in social studies, but role-playing can hardly be applied in the same way to mathematics or science. I suppose students could learn about geniuses in math or science, or even create a play about them, but this would not be the same as role-playing religious beliefs, especially when it includes reciting actual prayers. Besides, the principal did not say that the common teaching practices were used in other religions. As the Americans United noted, the Bible was officially banned from public schools in 1962 and school-sponsored prayer was banned in 1963. So whether a prayer is being actually recited or role-played to experience what it might be like to be Muslim, the prayer is banned and therefore should not be allowed in public schools, especially in the seventh grade.

Most people know that the transition from elementary to middle school is very important because it is such a formative time for teenagers when they begin to "find themselves" and develop important relationships. Regarding religion, many teenagers begin to rebel against or at least question the religious beliefs of their parents during this transition. Many parents reluctantly begin to allow teenagers the "freedom" they yearn for and eventually no longer require their children to attend religious services if that is the teenager's wish. Isn't it convenient that this is the time in a child's life that the religion and prayers of Islam would suddenly be provided? Apparently, the Muslim groups have noticed that this strategy of influencing young students in public schools is very effective, or perhaps liberal and Muslim groups have used the same tactics for years. Either way, seventh graders are very vulnerable and gullible at this time, especially when they respect and trust their teachers. Why shouldn't they, since their parents willingly drop them off at school and they are completely safe and secure? Not only do students trust their teachers to take care of them while they are at school, but parents trust the teachers as well. That is why students and parents are shocked when they find out that the schools are teaching them what can be considered religious orientation rather than the history about a religion.

World Net Daily reported that a parent of an Elk Grove, Calif. Junior high school student expressed shock when she arrived at the school and saw a banner which read, "There is one God, Allah, and Mohammed is his prophet". The WND article further reported that the parent, Valerie Moore, said that "They aren't just teaching about Islam, they are practicing it. They have them kneeling down and praying to Allah. I have a problem with that. That is more like inculcation". In the article, Moore also stated that she believed that part of the problem was the discretion of the teachers because the teacher spent four months on Islam and ran out of time before the section on the Reformation could be taught. To be fair to teachers, they likely teach what is at front of the textbook before they teach what is in the back of the book. If the teachers are not responsible for allowing religious education to go in the classroom, then who is, the Board of Education or the School Districts, the textbook publishers or perhaps Muslim groups that offer their assistance and contribution to what is going to be taught or not taught? If everyone knows that religion is such a hot topic in schools, then why not just teach the history of a religion? Could it be that Muslim groups do not want students to learn about their history?

Not everyone has a problem with role-playing activities taking place in public schools. Josh Gerstein, a reporter for the NY Sun, included the comments of federal judges involved in the Byron School District case. Gerstein quoted Judge Dorothy Nelson as she questioned those who are critical of the Islamic lessons in school, "Doesn't this seem more like a secular experience than a religious experience?" I don't know because I wasn't in the class or the courtroom, but if I was the judge, I would have asked the students what they thought and how they felt about the Muslim prayers and exercises. Isn't that what judges are required to do in family law court as the state's primary concern is the best interest of the children? Are the Department of Education, Board of Education, School Districts and teachers concerned for the best interest of the children they serve? Is not the physical, emotional and psychological well-being of each child the highest priority of all these educational agencies? If not, they should be!

Gerstein further quoted Judge Nelson as she questioned the critics, "Are you saying our children should not be taught the history of all the religions of the world?" I don't know what the plaintiff's attorneys were thinking, but this was their great opportunity to respond to the open-ended question. Obviously, that was not what the critics or attorneys were asking because that was not the complaint filed against the Byron School District. But since she asked, the attorneys should have told the judge that no school teaches the history of all the religions of the world nor are they required to do so. The teachers are only required to cover all the material and information according to the state standards. Although it would be nice to teach the students the history of all the religions of the world, everyone knows that there is not enough time to do so. However, since the school is teaching "about' Islam in public schools, perhaps they should teach about the real history, including modern and current history, of Islam and how the religion is still spreading across the globe. If students are taught about the actual history of Islam and how it "spread", including warfare and their goal to rule and dominate their enemies, then the students will be better equipped to realize that the war or struggle towards the goal continues to this day.

Why are the Muslims so afraid of telling the history of their religion? The judges, school districts and textbook publishers are allowing them to teach "about" their religion. Do they think that nobody knows about the history of Islam and how it spread? Why don't they want students to know about all the wars and violence that occurred as the religion spread? The history books tell about all the wars that have been waged by different nations and religions. There is no shame of being involved in a war, as long as there is a valid reason for it. Perhaps Muslims are ashamed of their wars or that non-Muslims will not perceive a valid reason for their current wars. Perhaps students will not understand why Muslims are still at war with and throughout the world since most modern wars are between nations or governments and not about religion. Perhaps students will not see the Islamic religion as a religion of peace as it has been described by recent American presidents. Whatever the reason may be for Muslims not wanting students to learn about the history of their religion, parents and concerned American citizens are waiting for an explanation.

Gerstein did quote another judge that seemed to have a different point of view than the other judges. Gerstein reported that Judge Carlos Bea suggested that the unit on Islam was more involved and more religious than other units on medieval culture. Although the court dismissed the suit against the Byron School District, the NY Sun article reported that no teachers in the district are currently using the Islam simulation materials, which were developed by a private publisher in conjunction with two Muslim groups, the Islamic Education and Information Center and the Council of Islamic Education. The use of such materials raises additional questions. For instance, how did the Muslim "educational" groups and the teacher know that the materials would be appropriate and satisfy the requirements of what needs to be taught according to state standards? Furthermore, how were the state standards written and designed to fit so well with the materials supplied by the publisher and the Muslim groups?

These same simulation materials were reported by Daniel Pipes in the Jerusalem Post in 2002. Pipes stated that students who follow the directions fight mock battles against Christian crusaders and other infidels. Pipes also states that following the victory, the Muslim warriors praise Allah. Pipes further states that students study the Koran, recite from it, design a title page for it, write verses of it on a banner, act out Islam's Five Pillars and go on a "pilgrimage to Mecca". Pipes also questions how the history of Islam is taught in the classroom as the curriculum states that the "Kaaba was originally built by Adam and was later rebuilt by Abraham and his son Ismail". Pipes remarks that this version of history may be an Islamic belief, but it is not verifiable history. The article by Pipes finally notes that the publisher of the Islamic simulation is Interaction Publishers, which gives credit to two militant Islamic organizations for their assistance. The article identifies the two Islamic organizations as the Islamic Education and Information Center and the Council on Islamic Education. Besides the questionable practice of having students recite Islamic prayers in American public schools, Pipes raises another key issue. Even if there were no Islamic prayers recited or Islamic exercises performed in schools as part of the state standard, is the history of Islam being properly presented in the classroom? In other words, is the actual history of Islam being taught to American students or are the students being taught a revised history of Islam? It is clear that the Muslim educational groups do not want the students to be exposed to the negative side of Islam's history, but the students are not even being taught with facts as the lessons attempt to glamorize and glorify the Islamic religion. Are not History and Social Studies scholarly disciplines just as the subject of Science is? Doesn't the American public school system want students to be taught facts about historical events rather than a slanted version that has been candy coated so that the students will view a particular religion in a positive light? I cannot say either way for sure, but let's take a look at a report that asks whether the presentation of Islam in America's classrooms is History or Propaganda?

The Mission Viejo Chapter of ACT! For America and the United American Committee created a special report that is titled, "Islam in America's classroom, History or Propaganda?" The report states that ACT! For America is a grassroots, pro-America, anti-supremacist educational and political-action organization dedicated to sopping Islamic jihad, terror and intimidation. The report also states that the organization was founded by Brigitte Gabriel, a Lebanese immigrant who came to the United States after losing her country to militant Muslim fundamentalists during the Lebanese civil war. I wish I could include the entire report here, but I will instead mention and discuss some of the key points of the report.

The very first item in the ACT! For America report is a quote from Joseph Goebbels, the propaganda expert and Reich Minister of Public Enlightenment and Education for Nazi Germany, which states, "If you tell a lie big enough and keep repeating it, people will eventually come to believe it". This quote has often been used in current political debates regarding many hot topic issues, but concerning the required practice of allowing Islamic prayers and religious exercises in American public schools, I think the quote is very appropriate because students are being taught a "nice and clean" version of Islam. I could use the term "whitewashed" but I don't want to use it simply because everyone else is. As I stated and asked before, why don't Muslim groups want students to learn about their real history and how actual events truly occurred? I know that no religion or nation is happy about the negative part of their history, but if it is going to be included in the created and required curriculum of American schools, then the actual history of Islam must be taught in the classrooms rather than omitting any negative aspect of the religion.

ACT! for America (ACT) states that the goal of the special report is to awaken educators, publishers, parents, the media and American citizens to the systematic deception about Islam that is being taught to middle school or junior high students. At the same time, the report states that Islamist propaganda is also a serious problem in American high schools, colleges and universities. In the introduction, the report also states that across the country many American schools are using taxpayer funds to promote a very dangerous form of propaganda, the misrepresentation of Islam. The report states that this is being done by textbooks presenting an overly benign picture of Islam as the textbooks never mention Islam's cruel history of atrocities and totalitarian ambitions for world domination.

Following the introduction is a historical note about the mandate President Bill Clinton gave to his Education Secretary "to provide every public school district in America with a statement of principles addressing the extent to which religious expression and activities are permitted in our public schools." The reports further states that the resulting document, "Religious Expression in Public Schools", provided an open door for Islam to enter American classrooms by stating that "public schools may not provide religious instruction but they may teach about religion" and also that "students generally do not have a federal right to be excused from lessons that may be inconsistent with their religious beliefs or practices." While I agree with the report that this document indeed does open the door for Islam or any other religion to abuse the permission of public schools to teach "about" religion, I am more concerned regarding the part which does not provide a choice for students to opt out of a lesson if the parent does not want their child to be subjected to religious beliefs or practices that are inconsistent with their faith or non-belief.

Although President Clinton's directive to the Secretary of Education appears to be consistent with the Supreme Court's definition of and rulings on the separation of church and state, I agree with the ACT report that Clinton's use of the term "about" allows room for Islam to manipulate the public school system, at least until their manipulation can be challenged and stopped by another Supreme Court. Any attorney or group of attorneys can use the same argument that was used by Schemp in the 1963 Supreme Court case and they will be able to prevent Islamic or any other religious groups from interfering with state standards, class lessons or textbook publications that allow misrepresentations or exercises of any religion to occur in the classroom. The book, Courts, Kids, and the Constitution, edited by Peter Irons, provides a relevant quote of Schemp's attorney, Henry Sawyer. Regarding whether reading from the Bible or reciting the Lord's Prayer is an establishment of religion, Sawyer states that "there is an establishment because the actions prefer Christian religions over non-Christian religions." After recounting Sawyer's argument, the book reports that the Supreme Court ruled in favor of Schemp and that public schools could not use the Bible and prayer for classroom devotion. The book then provides Justice Tom Clark's opinion on the decision. Justice Clark stated that "the place of religion in our society is an exalted one, but religion's proper place is in the home, the church, and the individual's heart and mind." The book further notes that Justice Clark remained firmly committed to a "position of neutrality" and that "the Bible is worthy of study for its literary and historic qualities in classes that do not involve religious exercises." The book also included a commentary on the Court's decision by a Catholic journal which praised the Court for protecting students against religious values that they do not accept.

I believe that all of these quotes and comments can be applied to the current practice of allowing Islamic prayers and reading from the Koran in American public schools, thereby rendering the practice unconstitutional. The current practice of including certain Islamic exercises and prayers in schools does show preference of the Islamic religion over non-Islamic religions, especially as it has been shown that specific textbooks have more chapters on Islam than on any other religion. In addition, it can also be shown that textbook publishers have shown preference towards Islam because the chapters on Islam are placed near the front of the books whereas the chapters of other religions are placed closer to the end of the books which may result in the chapters of other religions not being covered due to lack of time in the school year. Regarding Justice Clark's comments on the Bible as worthy of study, I would say that the study of the Koran would likewise be more reasonable in a college setting but not for students in middle school.

Following the notes about President Clinton's directive, the report provides definitions of history and propaganda. The report includes the Random House Unabridged Dictionary definition of history which states that "history is a continuous, systematic narrative of past events as relating to a particular people, country, period, person, etc., usually written as a chronological account." The report further states that in an academic setting, the term history means a scholarly discipline that is devoted to analyzing and reconstructing the past through the study of real events. The report then notes that this use of the term history distinguishes an account of actual events from an account of fictional events or people. Then the report includes a quote on the definition of propaganda by Garth S. Jowell and Victoria O'Donnell, *Propaganda and Persuasion*, which states, "Propaganda is the deliberate, systematic attempt to shape perceptions, manipulate cognition, and direct behavior to achieve a response that furthers the desired intent of the propagandist." Then the report continues by stating that the study of Islam by America's middle school students does not meet the academic definition of history, but the Islamic lessons perfectly fit the formal definition of propaganda. I wholeheartedly agree with the report's assessment.

Next, the report provides some examples of Islamic propaganda in public schools. The first example provided by the report is called glittering generalities, which occurs when the textbooks make statements about Islam that are unsupported by or even contradictory to historical facts, such as omitting the factual information about Islam's violent history of war, conquest and subjugation. The report states that students learn about how Islam spread to other cultures and lands, but not about its stagnation and decline. The second example of propaganda used in classrooms by Islamic groups is half-truths. The report states that in the textbook, *Across the Centuries*, students learn that "Mohammed stressed that women should be considered individuals with rights of their own" but there is no mention about women's second class status under Islam. The report then includes some teachings from the Koran and sharia law that describe their true thoughts on the position of women:

- Men are superior to women.
- Women are deficient in intellect and understanding.
- A husband has the legal right and religious obligation to beat a wife if she disobeys him, is disloyal to him or simply does not please him.
- A man may divorce his wife simply by saying, "I divorce you" three times. The woman will be removed from the household with no legal rights to visit the children or financial rights to any shared property.

Do any of these rules or teachings sound similar to the quote of Mohammed that is included in the textbook? The report then provides the next example of propaganda which is called, "The Big Lie". The reports states that students learn of Islam's tolerance and "multiculturalism" although they are not told that Mohammed said, "I will instill terror into the hearts of unbelievers, smite ye above their necks and smite all their fingertips off them." The report states that another big lie that is told about Islam in public schools is regarding jihad, such as when teachers tell students that jihad is "to struggle" against a personal evil like smoking when in reality, the term jihad means "Holy War" to spread Islam.

The next section in the report is regarding the vulnerability of children. The report notes that there are four primary reasons for their vulnerability:

1. Children do not have the knowledge or experience required for critical thinking. As a result, they are unable to determine if the information is true or not.
2. Propaganda is most effective when the information comes from a respected authority, such as a school teacher or school textbooks.
3. Children learn by example. So when a teacher speaks positively (*without any negative comment whatsoever*) about Islam, that emotional association is powerfully transferred to the students. Italics are mine.
4. Scientists have discovered that, because of the way our brains learn, once we develop an opinion or belief it is extremely difficult to change it.

I can attest to the validity of the fourth area of vulnerability. Actually, I am sure that most people can do the same since what we learn from our parents, especially regarding religion or politics, is very likely to become part of our belief or opinion for the rest of our lives, unless we endure a traumatic experience or encounter someone who is able to convince us that we need to think differently about some issue or topic. One common experience of mine was whenever I discussed the issue of religion with my friends or family, they would simply tell me, "I was born a Catholic and I will die a Catholic." Another unofficial requirement of being an American Catholic was that I had to cheer for Notre Dame in college sports, especially football. This "requirement" was easier to fulfill when the football team was doing well, but not so easy after Notre Dame began losing most of their games.

Eventually, I became a bible-believing Christian when I was almost forty years old. Despite hearing the scripture being proclaimed by a pastor at a friend's church week after week, I was still stubborn and did not surrender to Christ before reluctantly letting go of the church and traditions that I grew up with. I even attended a seminary college for two years as I considered entering the priesthood. Although I initially left the religious college because I wanted to get married, I left the church for a much more serious issue. Despite my love for the Catholic traditions and my best effort to be the model person, I could not find a solution to the problem of sin. I went to confession frequently, but no matter what, I continued to sin.

Realizing that sin can keep us from entering the kingdom of heaven, I began asking my fellow Catholics how we know that we will be allowed entrance into God's kingdom. Their responses were disappointing. The two most common answers were that I needed to pray more so I would get out of purgatory sooner or I could just "hope" that I will get into heaven. Needless to say, theses responses were insufficient to my inquiries. So finally my eyes were opened and I realized that Jesus died on the cross for my sins and that I just needed to accept his sacrifice on my behalf and I would be saved. Then the heavy weight was lifted from my shoulders as I discovered that Jesus already paid the price for my sins and I no longer had to worry about earning or deserving the gift of heaven. So as you can see, I can attest to how difficult it can be to change one's beliefs or opinions after learning so much during my childhood years.

The report also has a strong warning about how religious propaganda can be used and targeted towards children in public schools. The report mentions an article, "How to make America an Islamic Nation", that appears on the website, www.dawanet.com. The report quotes the article as saying, "Schools and campuses are no exceptions as places where Islam can be victorious. We should use every opportunity to sensitize non-Muslim peers and school staff to Islam and to establish an environment in which everywhere a non-Muslim turns he notices Islam portrayed in a positive way, is influenced by it and eventually accepts Islam. The report then states that this advice is in direct opposition to American laws which prohibit proselytizing for religions in public schools. So despite the ruling of the courts in the previously mentioned cases, the plaintiffs were not just falsely accusing or wrongly imagining that the public schools were being used for promoting the religion of Islam. Since this type of intrusion of the schools has been going on for several years, it appears the tactics of influencing and instructing students regarding Islam is intentional and not by accident.

This is exactly what the report says next by quoting another report by The American Textbook Committee, entitled, "Islam in the Classroom". The ATC report declares, "None of this is accidental. Islamic organizations, willing to provide misinformation, are active in curriculum politics. These activists are eager to expunge any critical thought about Islam from textbooks and all public discourse." The ACT special report includes another quote to support their concerns regarding Islam being taught in the classrooms of America. They quote former chairman of the board of the Council of American Islamic Relations (CAIR), when he stated, "Islam is not in America to be equal to any other faith, but to become dominant. The Qur'an should be the highest authority in America, and Islam the only accepted religion on earth." I suppose the next time a concerned parent wishes to pursue legal action to stop students from being taught Islamic prayers and exercises, the parent needs to call on these pro-American groups as expert witnesses to argue about the real intent of Islamic teachings and beliefs being introduced to public school students.

The next section included in the ACT report asks the question. "Who's behind the editorial revisions?" The ACT report quotes another report by the Textbook League which states, "Muslim propagandists owe much of their success to their skillful manipulation of publishers of instructional materials. They have been able to persuade various publishers to become their confederates, and these publishers have produced corrupt textbooks and curriculum materials which say what Muslims want them to say and omit any information that the Muslims don't want to see in print." The special ACT report states that the ATC has identified one Islamic organization, The Council on Islamic Education (CIE), as the group which has been the most effective in persuading textbook publishers to conceal Islamic ideology and to revise Islamic history. The ACT report also notes that the CIE's founding director is Shabbir Mansuri, a Muslim immigrant from India, who is listed as a consultant or a reviewer in textbooks or curriculum materials published by Prentice Hall, Glencoe, Houghton Mifflin and Harcourt Brace and Company. The ACT report further states that Diane Ravitch, PhD. Ed., who was Undersecretary of Education under President George W.H. Bush, wrote in her book, *The Language Police: How Pressure Groups Restrict What Students Learn*, "Three publishers [of world history texts] Glencoe, Houghton Mifflin, and Prentice Hall rely on the same individual from the CIE to review their Islamic content. This may account for the similarity of their material on Islam as well as their omission of anything that would enable students to understand conflicts between Islamic fundamentalism and Western liberalism."

Next, the ACT report considers whether a local school board is aiding and abetting the CIE's agenda. The report states the remarkable fact that CIE has been housed in the offices of the Fountain Valley School District in California since 1993 and that it has been discovered that the school board is starting the construction of a new building, which will include an office suite already leased to the CIE and its new front organization, The Institute on Religion and Civic Values. The report states that Shabbir Mansuri and his staff remain in charge of the group that has merely changed its name, and by doing so suggests that the group intends to conceal its Islamic agenda. This question asked by the report is a very legitimate one. Is the Fountain Valley school board ignorant of CIE's plans or is it willfully cooperating with CIE to promote the religion of Islam? I have to ask another question. Does the Fountain Valley school board or any school district in America have an office for any other religious group on its property? I am sure that no American school district or the ACLU is going to allow a Christian organization to have an office to promote its expansion. What do you think?

The conclusion of the ACT special report includes parts of an article written by Dr. M. Zuhdi Jasser, a Muslim physician who was the past president of the Arizona Medical Association as well as the current president of the Islamic Forum for Democracy. The report states that Dr. Jasser is widely recognized as one of America's few professing Muslims who are willing to speak out against the Islamist threat to America. In his article, "The Un-fought War on Islamism: To Stay Civilized and Free, We can't Be Ignorant", Dr. Jasser makes the following valid and disturbing points:

- "America's educational system has seemed unwilling to enlighten our children to the nature, history and implications of the war that has been declared on us and on free people in general by Islamist theocratic totalitarians."
- Few would deny that our nation faces a clear and present danger physically and ideologically. Over 30 attacks against American citizens from radical Islamists have been prevented by our security forces since 9/11."
- How will today's students ever be able to address this challenge to our existence in the next few decades if they never even had an opportunity to understand it?"

I think this last question is an excellent one. Can you imagine what would happen to many children if their parents did not teach or warn them about the dangers of fire and heat? What about the dangers of a swimming pool or a fast moving river? What about the dangers of walking bare feet in the backyard when there are nails or stickers around? What about the increasing danger of speaking to strangers or other people who attempt to lure children with candy or a little puppy? What about the real danger of texting a friend while driving a car? These are all real life dangers that children need to warned about by their parents. Why? Parents are responsible for the safety and well-being of their children. Likewise, when students are dropped off at school, the school becomes the responsible party for their safety. I know that this is a great and almost unbearable responsibility for schools. Nevertheless, the schools have a duty to fulfill on behalf of the parents and students. This duty is not merely to keep students safe during recess or when they are involved in a sports or recreational activity, but also for what information and material the schools are providing for the children. So why would schools allow such a risky and dangerous activity such as Islamic prayers and exercises when they know that the Supreme Court has banned such religious activities from being sponsored by the public school system? Why would the schools reason and think that Islamic prayers and exercises would be allowed and tolerated when Christian prayers and exercises are not? If the school boards and school districts want so much to teach "about" Islam because that is what President Clinton's directive allows, then teach about Islam's violent and terrorist tactics. Teach the students about Islam's violent and intolerant beliefs and rules. Don't just teach middle schools students that Islam is such a tolerant and peaceful religion when the real history and current events state otherwise.

In recent years, schools and other organizations have allowed female students and athletes to excel like never before. I commend any and all programs that encourage female students that they too can be or achieve anything they want. I know that this is not absolutely true, even here in America, but I am not going to be the one who stands in the way of a child who has great dreams

and goals. Are schools going to wash all the recent advancements
of female students down the drain by leading them into the trap
of Islam? I am sure there are many men who are on these school
boards and in leadership positions in school districts. Are these
men going to allow their daughters to fall into a trap by being
misled that Islam teaches respect and honor for women? Isn't
anyone going to tell all female students about the penalties of
honor killings and stoning that women can receive even though
the woman was a rape victim?

I hope that public schools stop allowing young students from
being taught or misled about the real dangers of Islam. I hope
that the schools stop this practice not only because it is illegal
and unconstitutional, but because all students deserve to be
told the historical truths about Islam and every other religion.
Whether Islam is given more pages than other religions is not
nearly important as what the students are being told about this
new and strange religion to America. Are schools going to teach
students about Iran and the hostage crisis? Are schools going to
teach students about how Islamic governments or nations treat
Christian minorities or minorities from another religion or tribe?
If public schools are going to make the very risky decision to teach
middle school students about Islam, then the least the schools can
do is teach the students about the real history of Islam instead of
teaching fabricated stories that make Islam look like someone's
gentle and wise grandfather who would not ever let anything
bad happen to his precious grandchild. Although God has been
banned from public schools, God is still going to hold the schools
accountable for what they are teaching His precious children. So
to all the school boards and school districts throughout this great
country, this warning is for you, "Be afraid, very afraid."

CHAPTER 3

Who is writing the textbooks for public schools?

When I was in junior and high school, I remember how the teacher always sat in the front of the class while the student's desks were all facing the front of the class. Thus, the students were facing the teacher and the teacher could always keep an eye on the students in case any student tried to disrupt the class. There was always someone who wanted to be the class clown, and that student would either throw something at the teacher or another student, or the student would try to sneak a note to another student across the room. Teachers did a great job of controlling the class and there were not nearly as many disruptions in the classroom as there are today. I suppose the main reason that the classrooms and many other things were more orderly back then was because students had more respect for the teachers.

Teachers should not feel bad because some students use their classrooms as an opportunity to goof off or otherwise demonstrate their lack of respect for the teacher. Students who tend to make trouble for teachers also make trouble for everyone else, especially someone who is in a position of authority. Perhaps that is why some people or organizations believe that they can take advantage of the students who have a rebellious streak or two. I remember watching young people dancing, drinking, smoking (different kinds of chemicals) and protesting against the war in Vietnam. After the news reports of the war appeared on television, there were the reports of young people in colleges, especially in Berkeley, calling for an end to the war. As a young child in junior high school, I did not understand what was really going on nor did I really care. Remember, all I cared about at the time was pretty girls and good music.

However, today I am better equipped to understand how protests are organized and executed. So maybe those students who were trouble-makers were not that bad after all. In other words, maybe a little stubbornness, resistance or unwillingness to do whatever everybody else is doing can be a good thing. In other words, maybe it is not good for everyone to simply go along with the crowd simply because it is the trendy or popular thing to do. For instance, is it a good thing that people are protesting in Syria, Yemen and Saudi Arabia simply because there were protesters in Egypt, Tunisia and Libya? Does anyone really know why all of these protests are suddenly occurring one right after another when there has been no visible protests in any of these countries for almost thirty years? Does anyone really know who is doing the protesting in each of these countries? Is it possible that one person or one group can be organizing all of these protests and other forms of uprising against so many governments all at once? Although the general public may not know the answers for some time, there is someone or some group who knows. Whoever this person or group is, they know how to motivate people and get the ball rolling. This person or group also knows that most people will do something simply because they are told to do so or because "everyone else is doing it".

This type of strategy is very effective when used with adults, so it is likely even more effective when used with public school students who are in middle or high school. Why is this strategy so effective, even in our sophisticated society where people are supposed to be more intelligent, enlightened and aware? Because despite living in an advanced and developed society where young people have their own cellphones, ipads and laptops, most young people do not want to be alone or seen as outsiders or anti-social. Therefore, most of these young people will do whatever they are told or taught to do. Most students may not want to do what their parents tell them to do, but they will not hesitate to follow directions when the directions are coming from a teacher or some other leader. Hence, when middle and high school students are presented with information, whether it is true or not, they are more likely to accept the information as being true. This point was mentioned in the last chapter as the ACT report stated that children and students are very vulnerable to deceptive tactics because they are simply following instructions provided by the teacher. Besides, isn't that what perfect and bright students are supposed to do, follow the directions and learn the material given in the class? Yes, that is precisely what model students are directed and expected to do. And that is exactly what certain people and groups are counting on.

The last chapter was about what is being taught in today's classrooms and what are the students learning. However, this chapter is about who is supplying the information that is being taught to the students in the classroom. This chapter also provides possible reasons as to why certain people and groups are supplying such information to American middle school and high school students. I intend to humbly attempt to demonstrate that the priority for textbook publishers of History and Social Studies books is financial success rather than historical accuracy and professional credibility. But before doing so, I would like to again express my sincere appreciation to courageous groups that reviewed the most used history textbooks in middle and high schools in America. I cannot overstate the importance of their reviews. I appreciate their courage and straightforwardness not only because I have used them as resources in this book, but more importantly because parents, communities, and every American taxpayer needs to know what type of information is being presented to young and impressionable students in the name of History.

The main group whose research and reporting has tremendously helped me to learn what is included in modern textbooks is The American Textbook Council (ATC). According to its website, the

ATC is an independent national research organization established in 1989 to review the history and social studies textbooks that are used in the nation's schools. The information regarding ATC's foundation continues by stating that ATC has achieved a prominent place in national discussion about history books and the social studies curriculum through its many studies and reports. The statement declares that ATC was founded on the premises that textbooks are powerful instruments of teaching and learning and that they constitute the de facto curriculum in most schools, but textbook selection at the district and school level is often a casual and haphazard affair and political considerations too often intrude on content.

The ATC website also provides review guidelines for education professionals to use in their selection of history textbooks. The guidelines include the following basic questions that educators should ask in their determination of which textbooks to acquire for their schools. Is the information accurate? Is the treatment of various groups in society fair and unbiased? What subjects are emphasized? What kinds of history are stressed? Regarding instructional activities and teacher guidance materials, the guidelines suggests additional questions. Do questions provided for students help them to analyze the information and to think critically; that is, to reflect, hypothesize, analyze, verify, synthesize? Do the students have the opportunity to discuss or debate ideas presented in the textbook? Can students generate their own questions? I believe these questions are practical and legitimate and that it would be beneficial to any educational leader, whether they be a teacher or superintendent, to ask such questions while considering which textbooks are going to be used in the classroom.

The ATC website also includes the testimony of its director, Gilbert T. Sewall, as he testified before the U.S. Senate Health, Education, Labor and Pensions Committee hearing on Intellectual Diversity in 2003. The following are excerpts from the testimony:

36

"Since 1989, the Council has identified many problems with history textbooks. Textbook content is thinner and thinner, and what there is, it is increasingly deformed by identity politics and pressure groups. The first history textbook problem is what educators, critics and journalists informally refer to as "dumbing down". Many history textbooks reflect lowered sights for general education. They raise basic questions about sustaining literacy and civic understanding in a democratic polity and culture. Bright photographs, broken format and seductive color overwhelm the text and confuse the page. Among editors, the phrase "fact-based" is a negative. A picture, they insist, tells a thousand words. This declining textbook quality is neither a right nor a left issue. Publishers are adjusting to short attention spans and non-readers. Too many children cannot or do not want to read history which contains concrete facts and complicated concepts. So textbooks become picture and activity books instead.

The second history textbook problem is that of increasing content bias and distortion and it involves political judgment. One person's distortion is another's correction. Yet the list of textbook activists grows. The list spans gender, ethnic, religious, environmental and nutrition causes that want to use textbooks to advance their agendas. A large part of the problem rests with the textbook publishers. Today, four defensive, revenue-driven multinational corporations – Pearson, Houghton Mifflin, Harcourt, and McGraw-Hill – offer fewer and fewer standard textbooks for states and teachers to choose from.

None of these publishing giants shows the least interest in innovation, change or offering books that come closer to meeting the wishes of textbook critics and state-level curriculum reformers. Instead, publishers cater to pressure groups for which history textbook content is an extension of a broader political or cultural cause. They make books in which the content is meant to suit the sensitivities of groups and causes more interested in self-promotion than in historical fact, scholarly appraisal, or balance.

The collaboration of educational publishers with pressure groups and textbook censors is disturbing. Determining what history children will learn, who will be heroes and villains, what themes will dominate, and what message will be sent are crucial subtexts in civic education. At worst, biased instructional materials are undermining student's appreciation for America and citizenship. Publishers should be producing cheaper books that are more text-centered, simpler in design, and more honest in content. They are failing to do so. The four giants in educational publishing are ignoring these efforts in order to maximize revenues."

The testimony of Sewall seems to indicate that the process of selecting which history textbooks to use in the classroom is tainted by politics rather than relying on historical accuracy that can be verified by historians and experts in a specific area or subject. However, as Sewall noted, there also seems to be the initial problem of what information is included in the textbooks. I agree that these concerns are valid and therefore need to be discussed and addressed by the public and by school officials. I will now examine one of several reports produced by the ATC to determine if Sewall is correct in his assessment of the current textbook selection process.

In its report, "Islam and the Textbooks", the ATC reviews several World History and Cultures textbooks that are aimed at seventh to ninth grade students and at tenth to twelfth grade students. The ATC identifies the textbooks and publishers as Human Heritage by Glencoe, 2001, Across the Centuries by Houghton Mifflin, 1994, A Global Mosaic by Prentice Hall, 2001, Patterns of Interaction by McDougal Little, 1999, Connections to Today by Prentice Hall, 2001, The Human Experience by Glencoe, 1999, and Continuity and Change by Holt, Rinehart and Winston, 1999.

This first report begins by stating how widely adopted world history textbooks cover Islam and why the history of the Middle East is a timely and important subject for students to learn about.

The report notes that the ATC's findings and conclusions rely on respected historians and standard sources, prominent articles and essays, and diverse bulletins. The report states that it will compare the content of these sources to lessons and textual passages contained in textbooks previously mentioned. Then the report states that the comparison revealed that there were content distortions and inaccuracies that have not occurred by accident, and that the lessons and the process by which they are put into America's classrooms raise serious concerns about the integrity of world history as a subject.

The report acknowledges that the subject of Islam is complicated and has captured the attention of teachers, professors, public policy experts and religious organizations. The report then states that few teachers have at their disposal anything more than a faint knowledge of Islam. The report continues by stating that nevertheless, state mandates expect or require them to teach something about Islam. The report then notes that how classrooms address Islamic aggression is an unresolved school-related question of great importance. The importance of such an issue is exemplified by the declaration by The National Association of School Psychologists which states that "history shows us that intolerance only causes harm. Some of our country's darkest moments resulted from prejudice and intolerance for our own people because Americans acted out of fear." I agree with the declaration by the NASP. Interestingly, intolerance acted upon by other groups and nations other than America can likewise inflict great and unnecessary harm upon the general population of the entire world.

The declaration by the NASP also raises a simple question. Is Islam a religion of tolerance? In other words, does Islam tolerate and consider other religions and belief systems as being equal to Islam, thereby acknowledging and recognizing that all humans have and deserve the sacred right of choosing their own faith, or the right to deny such faith? The report states that teachers and parents are urged to "discuss historical instances of American intolerance", such as the treatment of Japanese-Americans after the attack on Pearl Harbor and the backlash against Arab Americans during the Gulf War. This urging is also interesting because no organization in any of the textbooks reviewed urges teachers and parents to discuss any example of Islamic intolerance. Discussion of any instance of Islamic intolerance seems to be more important than any past American intolerance since Islamic acts of intolerance are ongoing and can affect almost any country or culture in the world. However, any such discussion, especially in public schools, is not likely to take place in the near future.

The report seems to be making the same point by stating that in the case of Islam, perhaps more so than other areas of social studies, these are lessons that skirt the reality of international affairs and threats to world peace. The report demonstrates that there is a double standard applied by schools when considering the intolerance of America and of Islam. The report indicates that there is a tendency for teachers to apologize to Muslims for the intolerance of Americans, but there is no such tendency to demand apology from Muslims when there is an example of Muslim intolerance towards Americans. The report mentions that U.S. officials have assured Muslims in word and deed that America is a tolerant and open-minded nation, and officials have stressed the distinction between apolitical Muslim citizens and a belligerent Islamic agenda, thereby avoiding the branding of Islam as the enemy. The schools and news media do the same thing, always making the clear announcement that most Muslims are peace-loving and that only a small minority are militant or extremists. Yet, no such statement is made when Americans are accused of racism or religious intolerance during political and social debates. In the previous statement made by the NASP regarding the treatment of Japanese after Pearl Harbor, there is no declaration that most Americans are peaceful citizens and that only a few are intolerant and prejudice. Thus, there is evidence that such a double standard exists in schools and other public agencies.

As the report continues, it quotes Fred M. Donner of the University of Chicago, who stated that "most Muslims in principle applaud the decision to present more material on Islam and Islamic history, but nonetheless, their approval is constrained by their own strong views on *how* this material should be presented." Donner further states that Muslims resent the suggestion that Islam is a "religion of violence", an image dating back to the Middle Ages in western writings. However, Donner explains that to eliminate such references altogether would simply be to replace the stereotype of a "religion of violence" with an apologetic view that Islam is an early form of pacifism. The report then makes the important note that what may appear to be a minor curriculum controversy has far-reaching implications for civic education and the promotion of U.S. constitutional values.

Next, the report states that since Donner voiced his concerns, the coverage of Islam in world history textbooks has expanded and in some respects improved. For instance, the report notes that the expanded coverage of Islam in the history textbooks offers students a detailed look at the Muslim world, such as explaining its origins and tenets, and focusing on Islamic art, science, medicine and knowledge through the centuries. However, the report states that on significant Islam-related subjects, textbooks omit and flatter, thereby preventing or avoiding criticism or harsh judgments that would raise provocative or alarming questions. The report then reviews how certain Islamic terms and issues are presented and defined in the textbooks.

Jihad

For instance, what is the definition for "Jihad"? According to the report, Jihad in its historical usage refers almost exclusively to armed warfare by Muslims against non-Muslims. The report also includes a quote from Bernard Lewis, writing in *The Middle East*, as he stated that the overwhelming majority of early authorities, citing relevant passages in the Koran and in the tradition, discuss

41

jihad in military terms. Lewis makes the point that almost every manual of sharia law has a chapter on jihad. Lewis further states that the Muslim jihad was perceived as unlimited, as a religious obligation that would continue until all the world had either adopted the Muslim faith or submitted to Muslim rule. Those who did not, Lewis continues, were given the option of conversion, death or slavery. The report then notes that Lewis concludes this passage by saying, "The object of Jihad is to bring the whole world under Islamic law." The report also includes a definition of Jihad in the 1999 Library of Congress report on global terrorism. The Library of Congress report states that the doctrine of jihad has been invoked to justify resistance, including terrorist acts, to combat "un-Islamic regimes, or perceived external enemies of Islam, such as Israel and the United States. These definitions of jihad appear to be appropriate and correct, considering many actions and statements that have been directed towards Israel and America by Arab leaders and terrorists.

However, the report notes that the definition of Jihad is very different in the textbooks that are used in American classrooms. The report states that according to a Council on Islamic Education (CIE) subject guide intended for publishers, jihad means "struggle in the cause of God, which can take many forms, such as obtaining an education, trying to quit smoking, or controlling one's own anger." The report also notes that a widely adopted seventh grade Houghton-Mifflin world history book, *Across the Centuries*, says that jihad is merely a struggle to do one's best to resist temptation and overcome evil. If this is the true definition of jihad, then no wonder Muslims appear to be so unhappy and angry on television, because I can attest to the fact that in doing my best to fight temptation and sin, I never succeed in overcoming evil on my own. The report then states that another textbook, Prentice Hall's *Connection to Today*, which names the CIE as an editorial reviewer, says, "Some Muslims took on jihad, or effort in God's service, as another duty." The textbook continues by saying,

"Jihad has often been mistakenly translated simply as holy war, but in fact, it may include acts of charity or an inner struggle to achieve spiritual peace, as well as any battle in defense of Islam." This last definition seems to be describing other religions that promote good works and self-growth, such as Buddhism or Hinduism. But if Muslims wish to perform good works in God's service, then they will not find any objection from me. I guess it depends on what constitutes good works.

The report does state that Glencoe's *The Human Experience* provides a better definition of jihad by stating that Arab armies were united in the belief that they had a religious duty to spread Islam and therefore, they saw their conquests as a jihad, or holy struggle to bring Islam to other lands. The report notes that the CIE is listed as a reviewer for this textbook as well, so the differences in the definition of jihad provided by various textbooks indicate that the editor still determines what information is to be included in a textbook. These comments by the report also demonstrate that the report attempts to be objective in its review of textbooks rather than merely criticizing and condemning all of the textbooks for their coverage of Islamic terms and issues.

Sharia

The next term discussed in the report is Sharia. The report again quotes Bernard Lewis, who states, "In an Islamic state, there is in principle no law other than the sharia, the Holy Law of Islam and there is no distinction between canon law and civil law, between the church and state law. There is only a single law, the sharia, accepted by Muslims as of divine origin and regulating all aspects of human life: civil, commercial, criminal, constitutional, as well as all things pertaining to religion." The report states that the CIE says, "this term refers to guidance from God to be used by Muslims to regulate their societal and personal affairs." However, the report states that Lewis understands the term differently as he states, "The principal function of the Islamic state and society was to maintain and enforce these rules." With all the increasing reports of honor killings in the United States and stoning by death in various Muslim countries, I tend to agree more with Lewis' definition of sharia. As a simple outsider to all the procedures that are part of producing a public school textbook, I would say that the CIE should abstain from further advising textbook publishers due to a conflict of interest.

The textbook, *Patterns of Interaction*, by McDougal Littell, defines sharia as a system of law that regulates the family life, moral conduct, and business and community life of Muslims; "it brings a sense of unity to all Muslims." Another textbook, *Connections to Today*, by Prentice Hall uses almost the same definition, but according to the report, distinguishes sharia law from Western law by stating that, "unlike the law codes that evolved in the west, the Sharia does not separate religious matters from criminal or civil law." This distinction is very important and, if true, provides the explanation why Islamic law and Western law cannot coexist together in the same country or nation. This distinction also makes one wonder why the ACLU would support the teaching and recitation of Islamic prayers in the classroom because the ACLU has always argued for the separation of church and state. If the religion of Islam and the Islamic state both enforce sharia law, then the practices and policies of sharia would be completely opposed to the U.S. Constitution which strictly prohibits any state or government support for or establishment of any religion. Again, I say, where is the ACLU and why are they not suing or threatening to sue all the school districts that are allowing Islamic prayers and recitations to be taught in public school classrooms? Isn't that what the ACLU tells Christian parents, to send their children to private schools if they wish to pray in class or promote their religion? What makes Islam exempt from all of the legal intimidation and actions that Christian students and parents are accustomed to receiving from the ACLU?

The report states that the textbook, *The Human Experience*, says, "Law cannot be separated from religion in Islamic society." This is a very dangerous idea and practice. This is also why the founders of America warned about the state establishing a religion, because religion is so important to its followers that anyone outside of the state religion would be persecuted and considered an outcast. This is exactly why the early Americans left England, because the British government and church considered all citizens to become servants of the government. In other words, when a state and religion are one, there is little concern for tolerance for those who disagree with such a relationship. So despite the call and demand for tolerance in public schools, there is little tolerance for anyone who disagrees with the school system and its policies. That is why it is so interesting to see the ACLU aggressively take legal action against anything Christian in schools while remaining quiet as Islamic prayers and spiritual exercises are taught to middle school students in American public schools.

The report supports my questions with its own question. "What aspects of sharia do most world history textbooks fail to convey?" The report asserts that the textbooks fail to convey that the Islamic state is an agent of religion and that separation of church and state, limited government, and the underlying notions of personal liberty and individual freedom, especially freedom of religion are alien concepts. The report continues by noting that due process and trial by jury are also foreign ideas to Islam. Then the report also describes the danger of sharia law because it can be a system of religion-based behavioral control in which certain crimes are punishable by stoning, amputation, beheading, and other punishments intended to inspire fear and subjection. Liberals and progressives usually criticize the U.S. justice system and oppose the death penalty because it is considered cruel and unusual punishment, but these groups that appear to be anti-American are likewise silent about the harsh penalties of Islamic law and enforcement. Are not the punishments previously mentioned considered barbaric and uncivilized? If so, then how can anyone who calls themselves progressive support a system that reverts back to the seventh century and even before that? Another question about the potential danger of sharia, can you imagine what would have happened if the Pharisees and Sadducees had the authority of Rome at the time when they were deliberating how to accuse Jesus of a crime punishable by death? I imagine that the Jewish religious leaders would not have needed to falsely accuse Jesus before Pontius Pilate. They would have simply put Jesus to death all on their own. That is how dangerous it can be when a state and religion are united against its citizens. Perhaps that is also why the ACLU has so strongly argued for the separation of church and state.

Slavery

The next term discussed in the report is slavery. The report states that Glencoe's *The Human Experience* ignores the controversial subject while Holt, Rinehart and Winston's *Continuity and Change* barely alludes to Muslim slavery in a passage, "After about A.D. 1100, Ethiopia once again began to export gold and ivory to Egypt, and African slaves to the Arab world." The report notes that Prentice Hall's *Connections to Today* is more specific by stating that slaves were brought from conquered lands in Spain, Greece, Africa, India, and Central Asia, but Muslims could not be enslaved. Those individuals and groups that constantly condemn and criticize America's founding fathers for not completely prohibiting the practice of slavery should keep in mind that nearly every country in the world, including Muslim society, practiced slavery long before the United States became a country. There is little wonder for the current and ongoing criticism of America's history of slavery as the report suggests that modern textbooks present slavery as essentially a European and American event.

While the report states that one such book, McDougal Little's *Pattern of Interaction*, presents America and Europe in a negative light due to the issue of slavery, it does state that this same book addresses the subject of Muslim slavery with facts and details, which no other widely adopted world history textbook does. The report states that in the section entitled, "The Atlantic Slave Trade", the textbook states that the spread of Islam into Africa ushered in an increase in slavery and the slave trade. The report further states that African rulers justified enslavement with the Muslim belief that non-Muslim prisoners of war could be bought and sold as slaves and that, as a result, between 650 and 1600, black as well as white Muslims transported as many as 4.8 million Africans to the Muslim lands of Southwest Asia. I commend this textbook for including such facts that may disappoint Muslim pressure groups, but if such information can be verified as actual history, then it should be taught as part of the history lessons. Since these events occurred many centuries ago, there should be no shame for Muslims today, just as middle school students (and all Americans) should no longer be blamed or feel guilty about events that took place many generations ago.

Status of Women

Next, the report discusses the very sensitive issue of the status of women in the Muslim world. While discussing this topic, the report mentions the contrast of how the textbooks have included women in history and amplified their accomplishments but have attempted to minimize or avoid facts or details concerning the treatment of women because such information might be unacceptable or alarming to American students. The report notes that the textbook, *Human Heritage*, includes the general statement, "Islamic society produced some women of great knowledge and power." This statement is interesting for two reasons. First, the passage does not mention any specific Muslim women who acquired great knowledge or power. Second, the women who have written about their experience as a woman in Muslim society, such as authors Brigitte Gabriel, Ayaan Hirsi Ali and Nonie Darwish, have described such experiences as being mostly negative and degrading. But then again, perhaps the Islamic world would not agree that these particular women had great knowledge or power.

The report then includes another interesting quote from the textbook, *Continuity and Change* by Holt, Rinehart and Winston, which states "although men had most of the power in Arab society, women had some freedom. A woman's primary role, however, was that of mother." Again, the passage includes no specifics, such as what type of freedom did Muslim women enjoy and what type of freedom were not given to Muslim women. Although most people in the modern world finally recognize that the unofficial position of mother is perhaps the most important and most demanding job in the world, I am not so sure that is what is meant by the statement that the primary role of Muslim women was that of mother. May someone correct me if I am wrong, but that statement sounds much more like the outdated saying that many American males used when they said that "women belong in the kitchen".

Next, the report states that the textbook, *The Human Experience* by Glencoe includes vague propositions and false claims, such as Islam did improve the position of women, the wives of Muslim men were treated as equals and with kindness, and that women had complete control over their property. According to the report, the textbook, *Connection to Today*, acknowledges that countries like Saudi Arabia and Iran have opposed the spread of many western influences among women. For instance, the textbook includes a quote by an Egyptian student who said, "I think of Muslim dress as a kind of uniform. I can sit in class with men and there is no question of attraction and so on—we are all involved in the same business of learning." The textbook also includes the statement that some women in Muslim countries were dismayed and these women argued against social and political forces that placed severe limits on their lives. I think that this type of information is to be respected and considered valuable as it presents two different views of how Muslim women feel about their religion. This type of equal or balanced presentation of various views in a textbook is far better than including only complimentary versions of a religion while omitting anything that might shed a negative light on it.

After discussing the somewhat controversial terms and topics, the report moves on to the interesting events which occurred in the state of Massachusetts. While the report includes reasons and situations which raise concern for American parents and students, there is one bright spot that gives hope that the battle over the questionable curriculum being presented in the classroom is not over. Educational leaders in the state of Massachusetts deserve a lot of credit for their courageous and determined resistance to pressure groups that enjoyed much success in other states. According to the ATC report, the state of Massachusetts revised its 1997 state history framework and the guidelines were criticized as being vague, obscure, complex or cryptic. Thereafter, the curriculum was attacked by activists who protested content that was Islam-related, labeling it racist and biased. The report noted that strangely, the protest did not come from Muslims but from Barbara Brown of the Boston University African Studies Center and Barbara Petzen of the Harvard University Center for Middle Eastern Studies. One may wonder why these two university professors would be interested in a middle school curriculum. A likely possible reason is mentioned in Robert Spencer's book, *Stealth Jihad*, as Spencer states that Harvard accepted $20 million in donations in 2005 from Prince Alwaleed bin Talal, a member of the Saudi royal family, to finance Islamic studies departments. Apparently, a large amount of money will not only influence what is taught in American universities, but in middle schools as well.

The report mentions that there were three main complaints registered during the public review process. The first complaint is "that the standards in grade 7 generally present Islam in a warlike manner, and that the focus is on violence and the clash between Islam and the West, and not on cultural and economic interaction." I suppose the activists did not consider that the violence and wars conducted by Islam is a form of cultural or economic interaction. I am sure that the university professors could not refute the actual violent history of Islam, but that is simply not the information that they or their donors want presented in the classroom. The response of the state was "that the standards appropriately refer to Islamic military expansion and to the important conflict between the Christian world and Islam." The response continues by noting that "one can avoid these subjects by inflicting inaccuracies on history." In other words, the textbook publishers could make the dishonest choice of including fabricated information or omitting the violent history of Islam because it sheds a negative light on the religion.

The second complaint, regarding high school standard WH15, is that the standard is insensitive and even racist. The state responded that the information contained in this standard is accurate and is taken from Bernard Lewis's *What Went Wrong*. The state response even quoted French historian Fernand Braudel who wrote in *A History of Civilizations* "that Islam failed to keep pace with Europe, that it has dropped two centuries behind Europe economically, and that it has to modernize." I suppose the activists could be correct in saying that this type of language is insensitive, just as it is insensitive to young sports teams that one team is the winner in a game and the other team is the loser. Or as some modern educators have proposed, that teachers should not tell students that they selected a wrong answer, but rather that the student should receive credit for selecting the best answer. I wonder if the same activists consider it insensitive that modern textbook publishers continue to label America as a colonial, imperial or oppressive nation. I wonder if the activists consider it racist that the publishers, the media and the institutions of higher education continue to criticize the United States for practicing slavery even though nearly every country practiced slavery as well. A common lesson in today's schools is that America became rich on the back of African slaves. I wonder if the students are ever told that slavery increased dramatically in Africa as a result of Islam's expansion into that area.

The third complaint is that standard WH57 refers to the establishment of the state of Israel in 1948 and standard WH64 refers to the "increase in terrorist attacks against Israel." Who knows why there should be any complaint about mentioning the historical fact and event of Israel becoming a state? Perhaps the reason is because most Arab countries do not recognize the state of Israel and vow to its destruction on a continual basis. Why aren't the activists crying out about insensitivity and racism when these countries state that their main goal is the destruction of Israel? Can anyone state the meaning of genocide? Does anyone wonder why some people are concerned that militant Islam has some of the same characteristics and goals of Nazi Germany? So again I say thanks to the state of Massachusetts for standing up to the activists from Harvard and Boston University in their attempt to influence the curriculum for middle and high schools. I suppose the Saudis tried to get a little more from Harvard for their $20 million, but it didn't work.

Although the pressure groups were not successful in Massachusetts, they have been very effective in other states. The ATC report points out that these groups have enjoyed so much success because of the political environment in education which calls for increased tolerance and sensitivity towards any groups or individuals who are considered victims of discrimination. Additionally, the report states that the multiculturalism movement allowed for an anti-American sentiment to take root in education and therefore determine how and what is going to be taught in the classroom. For instance, while middle school students thirty years ago were taught about the great success and achievements of the United States and Western civilization, today the students are taught that America enjoyed such success only because it exploited the labor of slaves and poor immigrants. As a result, the students, being good Americans, begin to feel guilty about such success and may even begin to question how their parents were able to purchase such a big house and drive a new SUV. So when the textbook lessons on Islam are presented to students, they do not question the validity or accuracy of the lessons, they simply feel sorry for the Muslims because Muslims have not enjoyed the same luxuries and amenities that Americans have. The lessons do not mention that most Muslim leaders and governments live in luxurious mansions while the rest of the population suffers in poverty and hopelessness. It is well known that the Saudi royal family lives like kings, but what may not be well known is that Yasser Arafat, the self-proclaimed leader of the Palestinians, accepted and kept millions of dollars from the United States for himself and his family. Thus, after Arafat died, the Palestinians continue to suffer in poverty while Arafat's wife and children live like the royal family in France.

Although not all Muslims, especially those in leadership, live in poverty, the strategy of portraying all Muslims as victims is very effective. Who would expect middle school students to question what they are being taught in a social studies class? Who can blame seventh and eighth graders for accepting all the lessons on Islam as being factual and true? Despite all the recent terrorist acts that have been committed around the world by Muslims, including 9/11, who can blame American students for wanting to be tolerant towards Muslims when they are taught that people discriminate against Muslims because of how they dress or because they come from another country to escape poverty and desperation. The students are not told that many Muslims who come to America are also trying to escape the Islamic governments that seek to control every aspect of their lives. The students are not told that women in Muslim cultures are considered property or that young Muslim females must cooperate with and surrender to the arranged marriage, regardless of how young they are or how old the groom is. Yes, many Muslims are victims, but not as portrayed in the lessons being taught in American public schools.

Many Muslim women and girls are real victims because of strict Islamic rules and law, but middle school students are not presented with such information. In fact, many Muslim females continue to be victims in America because their relatives, usually a father or brother, pursue them because the female has "disgraced" the family. As a result, the number of "honor killings" continues to grow in America while receiving little media attention. Perhaps the media follows the same policy as the school system by not wanting to offend anyone from the Islamic religion or report any news that may present a negative light on Muslims. This policy, whether it be official or unofficial, is very unfortunate and degrading because it implies that Americans are unable to handle any negative stories on Muslims or that only Americans are capable of senseless and grisly murders. Either way, when human life is taken away, the media should report it so that the readers will know that a violent crime has taken place.

Unfortunately, the textbooks do not include such horrible acts, but merely portrays all Muslims as victims because America is guilty of racism and Islamophobia. Hence, the report states that when anyone or any group criticizes or questions a Muslim about terrorist acts or gender inequality, the usual response is to state that Muslims are being stereotyped, persecuted or mocked. The report further states that when historians or foreign policy experts mention negative aspects of Islam, they risk being called an imperialist or a bigot. The report notes that the Council on Islamic Education (CIE), which is based in Orange County, California, takes advantage of the diversity movement. The report says that the CIE claims to act as Islam's liaison to America's public schools, but it is in fact a political advocacy organization that is funded by Islamic donors, perhaps even by foreign donors. Robert Spencer has written an excellent book, "Stealth Jihad", regarding American universities accepting funds from Saudi Arabia for the creation and development of Middle Eastern Studies centers, so I do not need to expound on that particular subject at this time.

CHAPTER 4

Are the media and others teaching Americans to hate America?

While I intended to include a chapter on how the media has increased the anti-America sentiment, even here in the United States, I will only mention a few examples at this time. First, the media has continued its anti-war and anti-America protests since the 1960's. As a result, a patriotic citizen must endure and overcome much peer pressure if he or she wishes to publicly display an American flag or any other item representing the USA. I know because I have been verbally taunted for wearing camouflage shorts or a USA t-shirt, especially right after the second Iraq war began. When I was attending a local softball game, I was literally booed as I entered the park to watch the game. I was somewhat surprised by the bold and verbal disapproval of my choice of clothing, but I simply ignored it because I was proud to show my support of the troops who protect this country and are willing to put their lives on the line every day. The media has been so effective in their denunciation of anything to do with the military, that many people actually believe that if one supports the American armed forces, then they must also support and defend torture.

However, the media has been amazingly quiet regarding military actions since President Obama took office. I am not surprised because the media is very quiet when the Palestinians and other Arab groups fire rockets at Israel, but when Israel retaliates, the media is quick to criticize Israel and often shows or stages pictures of children wrapped in medical tape. Of course, it is a tragedy whenever a child is injured or killed, but there is evidence of media bias when there are only reports of Arab children being hurt and no reports when Israeli children are killed. Another example of media bias against the military has occurred when it has quoted members of Congress as stating that the war is a lost cause or that soldiers are involved in criminal behavior before the facts have been told. The comments of Senator Murtha regarding the military missions and actions resembled the false testimony of John Kerry when Kerry accused his fellow soldiers of killing innocent people during the Vietnam War. In this case, I do not place the entire blame on the media, but if they were reporting and investigating like they are supposed to, then they would not print such stories that include exaggeration and fabrication. One can only speculate as to why the media would become engaged in such reporting, but biased or incomplete reporting does not help their credibility in the eyes of the general public.

Now I would like to share the comments of individuals and groups that have been reporting for years on the inappropriate and possibly unconstitutional lessons on Islam that are presented in America's classrooms. First, Stanley Kurtz stated in 2007 that "unless we counteract the influence of Saudi money on the education of the young, we're going to find it very difficult to win the war on terror." Kurtz said that he wished he was referring to Pakistani madrassas, but that sadly he was talking about K-12 education in America. Kurtz reported that the federal funds received by university Middle Eastern Studies programs under Title VI of the Higher Education Act allowed the Saudis to use the system as a Trojan horse and gain influence over K-12 education in the United States. Kurtz further states that Title VI requires the Middle Eastern Studies departments to pursue public outreach, but unfortunately there is no complete definition of what constitutes public outreach.

A staff report by the Jewish Telegraph Agency in 2005 states that Title VI was enacted in part for national security reasons. If that is the case, then someone in the government has dropped the ball because the consequences of Title VI have decreased rather increased the security of Americans, especially middle and high school students who are being misled or deceived regarding the threat of Islam. Both Kurtz and the JTA reported how the Saudis executed a well-developed plan of implementing lessons on the Middle East from their perspective into the classrooms of America. According to Kurtz, the first step is when the U.S. government gives money and a seal of approval to a university Middle East Studies center. The second step occurs when the center offers a government-approved K-12 Middle East studies curriculum to America's teachers (although in fact, the curriculum was bought and paid for by the Saudis). The next step takes place as the centers appoint Islamic leaders to speak at seminars for teacher training. The final step is when the teachers in America's public schools actually teach the lessons to students who are completely unaware and unprepared to challenge or question any of the material as biased, inappropriate or false. All the while, Kurtz states, the American government has provided little oversight to how the Title VI public outreach programs actually work or who is benefitting from such programs. However, someone in the Massachusetts Department of Education was observant and became alert to what was happening in the important education process and proceeded to write a report regarding the questionable practices and goals of the Middle East Studies centers.

In Kurtz's article, he reported that Sandra Stotsky, a former director of a professional development institute for teachers at Harvard and a former senior associate of the Massachusetts Department of Education, was present when the department was attempting to respond to the challenge after 9/11 by organizing seminars in Islamic history for K-12 teachers. The article then states that the department accepted an offer from Harvard's center of Middle Eastern Studies because of Harvard's prestigious reputation and the center was federally subsidized by Title

VI. Kurtz states that the department commissioned a teacher-training seminar designed to address important current Islamic issues, such as Islamic fundamentalism and terrorism, the lack of democracy in the Middle East, and the obstacles preventing women from obtaining legal and political rights in the Muslim world. However, Kurtz notes, the Harvard outreach program had no desire in discussing these issues.

Kurtz's article states that the Harvard center was resistant to the hot topics, so it was months before the seminar organizers agreed to include a book by Bernard Lewis. Kurtz reported that Stotsky was deeply dissatisfied as she requested seminars which included balanced discussions of modern Middle Eastern problems, but the seminars had a different agenda of promoting Islam as a religion and attacking America for its alleged prejudice against the Muslim world. The article then states that Harvard's outreach training encouraged teachers to design lessons that would present the life and teachings of Muhammad in a positive light, include exercises which called for students to "appoint imams", memorize Islamic principles and act out prayer at a mosque. According to Kurtz, Stotsky stated that if the Harvard outreach staff had designed similar lessons and exercises on Christianity or Judaism, the ACLU would have protested immediately.

Kurtz continues by stating that Stotsky became so upset regarding the Middle East Studies center's agenda that she published a report entitled, "The Stealth Curriculum: Manipulating America's History Teachers" under the auspices of the Fordham Foundation. (Interestingly, I was unable to locate this report on the Internet.) In the introduction of the report, Fordham Foundation president and education expert, Chester Finn said that "interest group and ideologues" have used the seminars to "fly under the radar" of ordinary curriculum safeguards, promulgating "bias, misinformation and politically charged conclusions, and never acknowledging their semi-covert agendas". Finn further states that these agendas often view "the history of freedom as

the history of oppression". In other words, the agenda is right
in line with the current propaganda slant used by the media as it
continuously describes the terrorist or militant groups as "freedom
fighters" and refers to Israel and the United States as "invaders
and occupiers". Strangely enough, this type of propaganda and
"reporting" is quite similar to the announcements by Al Jazeera
before and during the first Iraq war. While the Arab radio was
declaring that Americans were being defeated all over the country,
Iraqi soldiers were actually lining up to surrender because they
were ill-equipped, hungry and thirsty. I can also attest to the fact
that this pro-Islamic bias is rampant throughout most American
colleges and universities as the bias is evident when discussing any
issue in political science or current events. In one course I took
as an undergraduate, students read a book about the Palestinians
plight and daily struggles in the Middle East. The instructor
presented the material and argued that Israel and the United States
were to blame for all the problems Palestinians endured. Having
studied about Israel because of its biblical importance and its
new birth in 1948, I learned how the Jewish state was constantly
under attack from its Arab neighbors. I also learned that it was
the other Arab countries, such as Egypt, Syria and Jordan (and not
Israel) that were mainly responsible for the miserable conditions
Palestinians lived under. In 1967 and 1973, the Arab countries
told the Palestinians to flee and get out of the way because they
were going to destroy Israel and the Palestinians were going to
have the land after the military victory. However, as we all know,
the plans of the Arab countries did not quite actualize, so the
Palestinians were worse off than before. Not only were they used
as pawns in the wars against Israel, but the Arab countries would
not allow them into the other countries.

I quickly learned that this anti-Israel and anti-America bias
was par for the course in higher education. More recently, I had
another disturbing experience as a graduate student pursuing
my master's degree in education at the University of Southern

California. Although I am restricted from identifying the course or using any of the class materials, I can describe what happened in the class and how I felt regarding the lessons. The instructor called the course "Racism 101", but that was not the real title. She called the course by that name because the main purpose of the class exercises was to have all the students realize that white people have always enjoyed advantages, such as better paying jobs, nicer homes and a better education while minorities, especially blacks, suffered disadvantages, such as high unemployment, broken homes and a dismal education. Since I am Hispanic, I know that minorities may not have the same opportunities as "white" citizens, but I was never taught to be envious or resentful regarding the social climate in America. I was simply (and correctly) taught by my parents to respect all people, no matter their nationality or appearance, and to work hard at whatever I do. I was also taught to always thank God for everything! So I have tried hard to live by the standards I was taught, but I also learned as I became older that not everyone was taught the same thing. Most parents try to teach their children right from wrong and do so as long as they can or as long as the child is willing to listen, but after that, the children learn from school and their friends. Unfortunately, children can learn bad habits and information from friends who are rebellious and troublesome, but when students learn erroneous and misguided thinking from the schools, it is a tragedy and disaster. During the USC course I was taking, students read a book and other materials about racism. In one session, students were expected to empathize with the minority perspective and echo the anger against white people. The instructor asked each student to share their honest feelings. One Caucasian student voiced his honest opinion and stated that he was offended by the material and purpose of the class. I agreed with him, but I did not say anything until it was my turn to speak.

When it was finally my turn to share my opinion of the topic, I simply told the instructor and class that I was taught to respect everyone and that I basically agreed with Martin Luther King's dream, in that hopefully someday people would not be judged by the color of their skin, but by their character and actions. Actually, I try not to judge anyone because I know that I am a sinner and no better than anyone else. Therefore, I can be judged as easily as someone else. Anyway, the teacher could not believe that I had no racist beliefs at all, but I finally convinced her by informing of various times in which I was discriminated against, and I would never want to make another person feel the way I did. However, the teacher's pressure was intense and many of the students stated that they were either confused or guilty about the discrimination against blacks, even if they never were personally responsible for hurting anyone in any way, shape or form. I think they called it collective guilt and that meant that guilty or not, all whites were guilty. After the class, I felt very bad for some of my classmates, but I felt even worse for all the white students in the country that were being labeled as racist and arrogant and they didn't have a chance to defend themselves. So the universities are not only promoting an anti-America sentiment, but an anti-white sentiment as well. This is not good.

From my personal experience and the current political climate, where everything is controversial and no one wants to offend anyone (except Christians and Jews), I am not surprised that public schools have become a target for misinformation and propaganda. As Stotsky noted in her report, there is a double standard when it comes to allowing free speech and participation into the public square. For instance, Christians and Jews are forbidden to share their views and beliefs in public, but liberals and Muslims are allowed complete freedom to speak their mind and no one is permitted to challenge or question them.

Meanwhile, some traditions in America are considered to be sacred and some are not. Most people would think that Christmas and Easter would be sacred traditions but they are not, and now the school breaks are called winter and spring breaks. Apparently, the sacred traditions are held for Harvard and Georgetown universities. Although the original mission of both colleges was to promote the Christian faith and search for truth, now they are held in high esteem because of their academic and financial records. Thus, I am not surprised that American universities that are considered elite and superior would show more interest in donated funds than the pursuit of truth. Most people respect and appreciate Harvard, Georgetown and other universities for being around so long and for having such high standards in academia, but I am confident most Americans would be disappointed that such schools would in any way be an instrument of a biased or fabricated education in our public schools.

Some may ask for evidence that Harvard and others are accepting funds from Saudi Arabia to influence the design of educational lessons on the Middle East and Islam, so here are some facts and statements that anyone can investigate. In Kurtz's article, he states that the last piece of the puzzle was discovered by the JTA. According to the JTA, a little-known foundation called Dar al Islam (Abode of Islam) is located in Abiquiu, New Mexico. The JTA reports that the foundation was created with Saudi money and that it holds teacher-training programs. The JTA also reported that after the foundation's funding was discovered, some of the information on its website was changed. Despite this attempt to alter or hide financial information, there are other sources that are readily available. To commemorate the 50th anniversary of Harvard's Center for Middle Eastern Studies, Kurtz states that there was a volume published which identified the three specific sources of funding for the center as Title VI subsidies, matching funds from Harvard itself and funding from the Saudi-owned oil company, Aramco. Kurtz called the abuse of Title VI by the Saudis a Trojan horse. I think he was right.

In part two of its report, the JTA states that a Jewish parent, Dr. Murray Zucker, withdrew his son from public school in Santa Rosa, CA., because one of the supplemental materials,

"The Modern Middle East", included some questionable exercises. Zucker also stated that four Jewish students in a freshman class of thirty pupils felt "powerless, marginalized and unrepresented". Kurtz further reported that the complaints by the Jewish parents led to a published analysis of the material by a team headed by Jackie Berman, an educational consultant at the San Francisco Jewish Community Relations Council (JCRC). The report concluded that the Case Study of the Arab-Israeli Conflict included "historical distortion and factual misrepresentations and rendered it unacceptable for classroom use". The report further stated that the teaching materials are studded with "misinformation, manipulation, omissions of key facts, oversimplification of complex issues, historical inaccuracy and lack of context". As if the findings of Berman's team were not bad enough, the report notes such materials are paid for by taxpayer funds twice, once when the materials are purchased at the local or state level, and again at the federal level where some universities with Title VI Middle East centers produce, promote and endorse the materials.

Fortunately, there is a growing trend of awareness regarding the questionable material on Islamic history and culture being presented in the classroom. In the JTA report, Sandra Alfonsi, head of Hadassah's Curriculum Watch, is quoted as saying, "We believe we can no longer ignore the pattern of Islamist revisionism that leads us from the K-12 textbooks to university courses and demonstrations on the college campuses and to the issue of the infusion of Arab petro dollars that have funded and continue to fund American education." Jackie Berman of the JCRC acknowledges that the Council on Islamic Education has been very effective in influencing the textbook publishers. Berman states that the Jewish community "hasn't been at the table". However, the JTA report states that Berman's team has had an impact on some of the educational decisions being made in California. The JTA report notes that the curriculum commission rejected an Oxford University Press sixth-grade history program that Jewish and Hindu groups had criticized as biased, erroneous and culturally derogatory. As usual, it seems that it is permissible textbook publishers to include demeaning and false information on many cultures, but there is absolutely not to be any information that might offend Muslims or suggests that there are negative aspects to the religion or culture.

Another expert and author on the Middle East and Islam shares some of her strong and personal comments regarding the Islamic influence on American education. Nonie Darwish, who received fame overnight after getting involved in a heated debate on Islam on Al Jazeera TV, states in a FrontPage Magazine article that she is very disturbed by what is happening to education in America. In the article, Darwish mentions that she received an email from a concerned mother who stated that her daughter was traumatized after listening to an Islamic speaker in the class. The email noted that the speaker's name was Hassan Shibly. As it turns out, Darwish is very familiar with Shibly because she had debated Shibly's father on a Bridges TV program several years before. In the article, Darwish points out that the same Bridges TV was created to promote the idea that Islam is a religion of peace and friendship. Darwish states that the owner of Bridges TV decapitated his wife near Buffalo, New York. Darwish further notes that the goals of the TV station fit perfectly with the Saudi PR machine that is willing to spend millions of dollars to present a positive image of Islam, even if the information is fabricated and false.

Darwish included the email message in the article. The email stated that the pretext of the presentation was for Mr. Shibly to talk to the class about Islam and dispel some of the "misunderstandings" and "Islamophobia". The email further stated that Shibly told the boys and girls that the 9/11 attacks occurred because of America's blind support for Israel and the men who carried out the attacks were not Muslims, but atheists. That's an interesting point of view. I have never heard of atheists

being concerned with America's support for Israel. I know that
an atheist has been attempting to get God out of the Pledge of
Allegiance, but why would an atheist get involved in Middle
East issues where religion is the hottest topic of all? The email
continued by stating that Shibly spoke in defense of terrorism by
saying that terrorism is an example of people reacting with their
hearts and not their minds. The email then stated that Shibly
asked the question, "if someone insulted your mother, wouldn't
you retaliate against them?" Reflecting on the words of Shibly,
is he saying that Muslims react entirely based on emotions and
without reason or thought? And yet Shibly and others are trying
to get to the minds of young Americans by feeding them false
information. Actually, what is worse than false information is
omitting information that is needed so the students can decide
for themselves if a cause is meaningful or senseless.

Later in the same article, Darwish stated that the mother of
the student expressed outrage that the speakers were invited to
the school to indoctrinate underage, impressionable minds with a
hate-filled ideology and a hidden agenda. Darwish stated that she
was speechless after reading the mother's email. She further stated
that she was outraged and had heard similar stories from mothers
in California. Darwish said she wanted to tell all the worried
mothers of America to stand up against this kind of "education"
and that everyone must speak out before the indoctrination strikes
at the heart of America. I am so glad that Darwish and the others
have been speaking out regarding the Islamic infiltration into
America's public schools. Darwish has been there and knows
about the real threat and danger of Muslim propaganda. In
the article, Darwish noted the contrast of information that is
being disseminated. She said that while mainstream mosques
and Muslim leaders around the world are shouting jihad, death to
America, death to the Jews, and encouraging Muslims to conquer
the West, American children are taught that if they fear such
threats, then they suffer from Islamophobia.

This last comment brings up an interesting point. Everyone knows that a phobia is a type of irrational fear of something, like spiders, ants, bats or bees. Although one of these might injure a person who is allergic or if the spider is poisonous, most people are not likely to be harmed by the creatures. However, if a person, place or country is actually being threatened by an individual or group of people who cry out for its demise and destruction, then it seems to me that the fear (or concern) is not irrational. There is an excellent presentation on Islamophobia on Fora.tv sponsored by the Hudson Institute. The first main speaker, Anne Bayefsky, does an outstanding job of sorting out the facts from the talking points of Islamic propaganda. This is exactly why I wrote this book and the type of public debate that should be taking place in America's schools, especially in "higher education". However, if the information being presented in American classrooms is biased in any way, with no opportunity for questions or challenges, then there is no debate or search for truth. What kind of education is that? Is that what taxpayers are paying for? Do American parents want to spend $30,000 or more per year to have their children receive an education prepared for them by a Saudi-funded political group?

Before I finish, I just want to mention another hero of mine. David Horowitz, speaker and author of many valuable books on what is going on at universities throughout America, is one of the most courageous and intelligent people I have heard who is not afraid to say what is on his mind. Horowitz has been and is currently speaking out at universities regarding the threat of Islam. At each campus, he is verbally attacked and challenged, but he is well-prepared for each question because he has experienced many protests before. Parents of schoolchildren should search the internet for one of his speeches at a university campus and learn how to argue and refute people that are trying to suppress the freedom of speech that Americans cherish. If students cannot speak their views and defend their country, especially at a school in their own country, then the doors of all campuses should be closed so parents can invest and spend their hard-earned money on something worthwhile.

Lastly, this deceitful intrusion into the American school system by foreign interests and foreign enemies is cowardly, since the key target is middle school students who are not yet prepared for deciphering vital information, especially when that information may determine whether they are willing to fight and defend their country in the future. Why aren't the students being taught about all the good things being done by this country, such as its generosity and compassion for people who are suffering around the world from natural or "man-made" disasters? Why aren't the students asked to consider why refugees and others come to America from all over the world to escape from their home country? I hope and pray that many others like Horowitz and Brigitte Gabriel will answer the call to stand up against those who are trying to teach our children to hate America. God bless all the students in America and all over the world. May they be taught to love and not hate. May they be taught to respect each other and that bullying is wrong, whether it is done by children or adults. God bless the United States military for their courage and sacrifice. Amen.

Notes

Chapter One

1. Avatar. (James Cameron). (2009)
2. Kaveney, R. (2010). Avatar. [Review of movie directed by James Cameron].

Chapter Two

1. Egelko, B. (2003, December 12). Judge OKs Islamic role-playing in classroom. SFGate. Retrieved from http://www.sfgate.com
2. Americans United. Brochure entitled, *Prayer and the Public Schools.* Retrieved from http://www.au.org/resources/brochures/prayerinpublicschools
3. Abington Township School District v. Schempp, 374 U.S. 203 (1963)
4. Lynne, D. (2002, January 16). Islam studies spark hate mail, lawsuits. World Net Daily. Retrieved from http://www.wnd.com/news/article
5. Lynne, D. (2002, February 19). Book publisher: No Muslim bias. World Net Daily. Retrieved from http://www.wnd.com/news/article
6. Gerstein, J. (2005, October 20) Christian Families Sue Over School's Islam Role-Playing. New York Sun. Retrieved from http://www.nysun.com/national/christianfamiliessueoverschoolsislamroleplaying
7. Pipes, D. (2002, July 3). 'Become a Muslim Warrior'. Retrieved from http://www.danielpipes.org/430/becomeamuslimwarrior

8. A Special Report. (2009, January 28). Islam in America's Classrooms, History or Propaganda? Presented by ACT! for America, Mission Viejo Chapter and the United American Committee, Truth in Education Joint Subcommittee. Retrieved from http://www.actforamerica92691.org

9. Irons, P. (2000). School District of Abington Township v. Schempp. Courts, Kids, and the Constitution (pp.8-9). New York: The New Press.

10. Sewall, G. (2003). "Islam and the Textbooks". A report of the American Textbook Council.

Chapter Three

1. www.historytextbooks.com   Directs reader to American Textbook Council.

2. American Textbook Council. Independent New York-based research organization established in 1989.

3. Sewall, G. (2003). "Islam and the Textbooks". A report of the American Textbook Council.

Chapter Four

1. Kurtz, S. (2007, July 25). Saudi in the classroom. Retrieved from http://www.nationalreview.com/articles/221607/saudiclassroom

2. Jewish Telegraph Agency Staff Report. (2005, October 25). Tainted Teachings, What Your Kids are Learning about Israel, America, and Islam, Parts 1 through 4. Retrieved from http://www.campuswatch.org

3. Darwish, N. (2010, February 18). Islamic Indoctrination vs. Education. Retrieved from http://www.frontpagemag.com/2010/02/18/islamicindoctrinationvseducation